THE BREAKTHROUGH BATTALION:

Battles of Company C
of the
133rd Infantry Regiment

Tunisia and Italy
1943-1945

by Col. Richard F. Wilkinson

Published by Col. Richard F. Wilkinson
175 Queen's Drive West
Williamsburg, VA 23185
(757) 229-0165

Printed by McNaughton & Gunn, Saline, MI

First edition printed in the United States of America

ISB # 0-9770223-0-7

* *

Dedicated to the Soldiers of Company C

133rd Infantry Regiment

who served their country every day with valor

and honor during their many battles

in World War II

* *

Table of Contents

Foreword

This book tells of the exemplary combat leadership of Col. Dick Wilkinson, Virginia Tech Corps of Cadets Class of 1942. In the Virginia Tech Corps of Cadets, our mission is to produce leaders of character. Our vision is to graduate leaders who have the highest standards of integrity, leaders who are committed to the university's motto, *Ut Prosim* (That I May Serve). The foundation of our effort to graduate leaders of integrity is the cadet honor code: "A cadet will not lie, cheat, or steal, nor tolerate those who do." Cadets also learn moral integrity: treating everyone with dignity and respect, treating everyone as a valuable member of the team. Additionally, they learn that professional competence—thoroughly knowing one's job, abiding by the rules, and enforcing the standards—will be part of their personal integrity from the day they enter the corps of cadets. Commitment to service is demonstrated by the fact that roughly 80 percent of each graduating class of cadets are commissioned as officers in the armed forces. As you read this book, you will learn that Col. Wilkinson exemplifies aggressive leadership, character, integrity, and selfless service. While the book describes his superb performance as a combat leader during World War II, these qualities will provide the roadmap to success for every young man and woman setting out on a career today.

Dick Wilkinson's aggressive leadership in World War II was founded on professional competence and the courage to constantly press the attack. Development of Dick's professional skills began at a very early age; when he was eleven years old, his mother took him to the Gettysburg Battlefield and taught him the importance of controlling the high ground. As they walked the battlefield, she pointed to Little Round Top Mountain and told Dick to take the high ground and to hold it. Dick ran to the summit, and in his imagination, he deployed his soldiers in defensive positions. Then he ran back down to where his mother was standing and immediately learned an important lesson about following orders precisely. "I said to hold the high ground," she told him. "You get back up there and hold Little Round Top." As you will read in this book, Dick never forgot his mother's lesson on the importance of holding the high ground. His professional development continued as a member of the Virginia Tech Corps of Cadets. Here, Dick lived in a regimented military organization; upheld the cadet honor code; observed leaders, both good and bad; and then had the opportunity to lead other cadets. He also developed his skills with tactical weapons and learned infantry tactics. Recently, Dick's wife, Margaret, said, "I was never worried about him when he was in combat because I knew that he had wonderful training in the Virginia Tech Corps of Cadets."

The competence he gained as a cadet was complemented by extraordinarily sharp combat instincts that repeatedly saved lives and won battles. One day, as his entire division advanced abreast toward a German stronghold in Tunisia, Dick had a strong and sudden premonition to save his men by ordering them to hit the dirt. He acted quickly without the slightest hesitation, even though the only sign of danger was in his own mind. As soon as his troops were protected, German artillery shells exploded all around them. Men from other companies were killed and wounded. But because of Dick's amazing combat instincts, his troops were uninjured.

Dick's courage in combat was based on his aggressive and succinct philosophy: attack, attack, attack. This philosophy was bolstered by strong faith in the combat skills and bravery of his troops. During one battle, his company and another company were ordered to attack German defensive positions guarding a key rail line. Dick's company was eager to initiate the attack but the signal to go was delayed repeatedly. Finally Dick learned that the other company would not be in the attack. Knowing that his own troops were ready, and having full confidence in their ability, Dick obtained permission from his commander to launch the attack with just one company. He quickly routed the German defenders and secured the rail line with just half of the combat power originally assigned to the operation. As further evidence of his combat courage, you will read of several engagements won by Dick's company because he combined initiative and bravery to trick the Germans into thinking that he was leading a much larger force. Repeatedly German units surrendered or retreated, not knowing that they outnumbered Dick's company.

The author repeatedly demonstrates impeccable character and

integrity. He shows great respect and compassion for his opponent, the German soldier. He writes of his admiration for the bravery and professional skills of British officers and their men. Typical of his personal modesty, he constantly praises the courage and skills of his soldiers. He proudly reports that his battalion earned the Presidential Unit Citation for defeating a German force that was defending Mount Venere in Italy. There were three key reasons for this significant success: Dick was placed in command of the battalion; he planned the attack; and his men of Company C won the battle by climbing the mountain in the dark, maneuvering to the rear of the Germans and defeating a much larger German force. Every one of the many battlefield victories related in this book demonstrates that Dick's success as a leader is based largely on the absolute trust that his men had in his abiding concern for their welfare and on their unwavering faith in his professional judgment and planning skill. Finally, his deep sense of integrity is demonstrated by his diligent efforts to make the manuscript as factual as possible. In addition to his two trips to revisit the battlefields about which he writes, he has read extensively for many years on the battles he fought on those fields.

The author and his soldiers are models of selfless service. Repeatedly he volunteered to take the highest mountain and to lead the toughest fight. He has dedicated this book to the soldiers of his company for serving their country with valor and honor. He states that the story of his soldiers' selfless sacrifices must be told so that future generations will learn the lesson that sacrifices of self to the common cause are absolutely required. In this case, Dick Wilkinson and the soldiers of Company C of the 133rd Infantry Regiment were fighting for the liberty and freedom that we enjoy today.

Dick Wilkinson led his troops to success in defeating the German army and preserving our freedom. His book provides the roadmap to success for our nation's future leaders via aggressive leadership based on competence and courage, impeccable character and integrity, and a constant commitment to selfless service.

Maj. Gen. Jerry Allen, USAF (Retired)
Commandant, Virginia Tech Corps of Cadets

A Note from the Author

Let me explain how I went about writing this story. Fundamentally, I have written about each encounter at two stages of my life. After much study, thought, and soul searching over the years about what happened, I have written a basic dialogue of each battle. These are my accounts of these events as I recall them. Even today, some sixty years later, I remember many events in detail. I do not intend to gild the story in any manner—even at my advanced age. I trust that I am guided by truth, and I believe that I have high standards for truth. I have checked time and time gain with other participants to obtain their recollections of events, which provided me with a good check and balance system.

One of my guiding principles was to return to every battlefield in the company of several other comrades in arms so that we could review the terrain and obtain, as much as possible, the enemy's perspective of our actions. We found much evidence of enemy positions and of routes we followed, and we experienced the strain of once again climbing the many mountains we took and recalling where individual actions occurred. I am indebted to these soldier-veterans—Everett Cornelius (Texas), Eldon Johnson (Iowa), and Leighton McKeithan (North Carolina), who accompanied me to Italy in 1984, and to Robert Woodford (Iowa) and Wesley Gallup (Minnesota), who accompanied me to Tunisia in 1995.

On behalf of my comrades, I render our deep respect for our foe on the battlefield. We know we shared the same hardships and pains—and, perhaps, some of the same degree of repulsion for the war in which we found ourselves. The German soldier was a skilled, methodical, and well-armed opponent and fought with tenacity and courage. And, just as we Americans were, the German soldier was separated from his home and the people he loved.

On many occasions, we took Germans as prisoners of war. At first, we were tough and demanding. But in a bit of time, we offered the Germans cigarettes and sat and smoked together—with smiles on most faces.

I should also mention the role my mother (1887-1957) played in preparing me for battle. In 1933, she accurately predicted that in ten years, Hitler would try to take over the world and that I would be battling his soldiers. To get me ready for what she knew I would face, she took me—twice—to Gettysburg Battlefield and instructed me to take—and hold—the high ground there. I never forgot what she taught me, and it became my focal point in battles in Tunisia and Italy.

Acknowledgments

Writing a book is seldom—if ever—the effort of a single person. Nor is this one. Without the assistance of several men with whom I served in World War II, I could not have filled in some of the gaps in my memory of what we endured sixty years ago. While I garnered information from a number of sources, I owe a particular debt of gratitude to Everett "Corny" Cornelius, Eldon Johnson, Leighton McKeithan, Robert Woodford, Wesley Gallup, Robert Wessels, and Harry Davidson.

And I should acknowledge Frank "Snuffy" Graham, who dodged bullets and mortars to deliver our mail on the battlefield. I don't think I will ever forget him or his battle-weary jeep.

I also want to acknowledge the encouragement and help I received from Virginia Tech's Gen. Jerrold P. Allan, Col. Rock Roszak, and Col. David Spracher, and I would be remiss if I did not thank my editor, Clara B. Cox, and designer, Glen Duncan.

But my deepest appreciation goes to my wife, Margaret Walton Wilkinson, whose encouragement and support during more than sixty years of marriage have enhanced my life and made it possible for me to spend many hours conducting research, visiting battlefields, and writing this book.

Introduction

What follows is the story of a single infantry rifle company in action in World War II. As you read this account, remember that the men of the company accomplished not just the deeds described here but many more that led the Allies to victory.

The story recounts the actions of a very brave force that was called upon, time and time again, to attack! attack! attack! Often these attacks were directed at an opposing German force of equal or larger size, an enemy that was powerful and skillful in defending non-hastily-built defensive fighting positions in mountains and on high hills.

The story of Company C of the 133rd Infantry Regiment, 34th Infantry Division, needs to be told. As Americans, we need to remember what, when, how, and why the brave men in the ranks engaged the enemy in many actions. We should know about and better understand the great sacrifices made on numerous battlefields during this great war. We need to leave a record so that future generations will know that sacrifices of self to the common cause of liberty and freedom are an absolute necessity if we are to maintain that liberty and freedom. To put that in perspective, imagine that our country, the United States of America, lost World War II. The results would have been devastating to our institutions, to our very way of life, and even this story could only have been told in a language other than the English we speak today.

The infantry! Napoleon called the infantry the "Queen of Battle!" Successful infantry movements seize and defend land spaces held by an enemy. These seized spaces deny the enemy the space and infrastructure to conduct war and, conversely, provide the victor with the space and infrastructure to destroy the enemy's will to succeed.

Main Paths and Movements

Let us trace the main path and movements of the 34ᵗʰ Infantry Division from 1941 to 1945.

1941: The division was a National Guard unit that was mobilized with a muster date of 10 February 1941. The men of the division mustered in the states of Minnesota and Iowa, with most of them coming from Iowa.

Approximately 8,000 men, who formed the division, were sent to a new camp, Camp Clairborne, in Louisiana. About two months later, additional new troops were introduced into the division to bring it up to wartime strength of approximately 12,000. These new troops, like the men they joined, were fine, dedicated soldiers who came from the Midwest states from which the division had originated.

The mix worked well, providing the division with a strong base of men who were never recadred to form other new units, although that was a common practice in the U.S. Army. These men met responsibilities that had been passed to them through examples set by their parents, broader family units, and communities. They felt a keen accountability to their peers in the service of their country and the folks back home. They knew they had come from solid homes, families, schools, and churches. And they were loyal to their native land and its culture.

1942: The 34ᵗʰ Division did well in training in 1941 and was selected soon after the Japanese surprise attack on Pearl Harbor on 7 December 1941 to be the very first division deployed to Europe. On 26 January 1942, the 133ʳᵈ Infantry Regiment was the first to land, arriving in Ireland after crossing the cold North Atlantic Ocean, which was filled with peril posed by the superior strength of enemy submarines. The 1ˢᵗ Battalion landed with Company C in its ranks, the first combat unit of the Army to land in Europe.

Combat training in Ireland was strenuous and realistic, but Irish bogs and mud offered a surrealistic setting for troops preparing for desert warfare. The deserts of North Africa were, surprisingly so, the next call, and a major element of the division made an amphibious assault to seize the capital of Algeria, then called Algers, in November. By the end of the year, the entire division had arrived in Algeria and was preparing to enter Tunisia to engage in warfare with Gen. Erwin Rommel's German Afrika Corps, often described by experts as the best fighting infantry tank force in the world.

1943-1945: The 34th Division fought heavy battles in Tunisia and Italy. In the desert area of Central Tunisia, the division initially fought as a unit and completely repelled the initial strong German attack (February 1943) at Sbiba Gap, forcing Gen. Rommel to halt his main attack there; after three days, he turned forty miles to the southwest and attacked at Kasserine Pass. He was successful against two other U.S. divisions in penetrating that pass. Later, the 34th Division, along with other strong American and British divisions, counter-attacked, forcing the Germans to surrender at Tunis. The German loss of approximately 270,000 men was the first significant defeat the Germans suffered against U.S./British land forces.

In late summer 1943, the 133rd Infantry landed as a reserve regiment of the amphibious landing force at Salerno Beach in southern Italy.

The 34th Division became the only U.S. division to fight in Italy all the way from the landing in the south to the extreme northern border of Switzerland.

The war ended in May 1945.

Statistics

The 34th Division broke records in World War II. It faced more days of combat (517) than any other U.S. division, Army or Marine. It took more defended mountains and high ground than any other U.S. division.

Casualties for the division totaled 21,362, but enemy casualties were much greater—I would estimate eight to ten times greater, maybe more.

1

The Battle of the Kasserine Pass Area
Tunisia, 1943

Background

The area where the Battle of the Kasserine Pass was fought is square and measures 100 miles on all four sides for an area of 10,000 square miles, about the size of the State of Vermont.

The battlefield is a desert area with little vegetation—bare valleys and mountains—making the site resemble the surface of the moon.

Along the entire east side of this battle area lies a solid range of mountains that runs north to south and on the entire west side lies an even wider and deeper range of mountains that runs in the same direction. Between these two ranges lies a rolling valley, some thirty to forty miles wide.

Each of the two mountain ranges has two main passes, about forty miles apart on each mountain, that allow entrance or egress from the valley. Two passes lie in the east; two in the west—Kasserine Pass and Sbiba Gap.[1] These passes in the west were the key to all military movements of all forces.

About six maneuver divisions—and their support—occupied that site at the time of the battle. Each side, Germany and the United States, had the equivalent of three divisions. The Germans had two panzer, or armored, divisions and a third mobile force; the Americans had one armored division and two infantry divisions.

---

[1] *A gap is a very wide pass.*

The battle itself lasted for almost two weeks, beginning on 13 February and ending on 24 February.

The German's broad military objectives were to destroy the U.S. forces that were deployed along the east range of mountains[2] and seize territory deep within the U.S. positions by attacking in a northwest direction, to seize supply positions, and then to turn north toward Tunis[3] to force the northern-deployed British forces to leave Tunisia. Although they would adhere to their basic plan, the German generals, including Rommel, argued over details of what they should do as they moved to the northwest or north.

The broad military objectives of the U.S. were to hold on to positions in the eastern range,[4] although the U.S. was forced to fall back from that range to defend positions in the western range of mountains, and to defend the western mountains at all costs.

The Battle
14-15 February

The German side, commanded by Field Marshal Rommel, seized the eastern dorsal Faid Pass area on 14-15 February, inflicting heavy U.S. losses. By 16 February, U.S. forces had moved back to the western range[5] area. The Germans moved toward Sbiba Gap, not Kasserine Pass, with their main effort, the shortest and most direct course of action for them to take to reach a pass and the shortest and best avenue of attack to gain access deep within the U.S. forces and its rear areas, principally LeKef, a key logistical and administrative hub seventy-five miles into the Allied line.

These actions set the stage for the 34th Infantry Division to enter the picture. In retrospect, we know that the division arrived in the battle area just in time and on 16-17 February

---

[2] *The purpose of this objective was to prove to the world Germany's superiority over the United States.*

[3] *Tunis is 100 miles from the battlefield.*

[4] *Dorsal.*

[5] *Dorsal.*

was quickly focusing on the defense of Sbiba Gap. The other two U.S. divisions were concentrating on defending Kasserine Pass, forty miles to the southwest of Sbiba. Surely Rommel was tempted to attack the single U.S. division[6] that had not been tested in battle rather than attack two battle-tested divisions.[7] If he was tempted, that temptation won out—he attacked Sbiba, not Kasserine.

16 February

On 16 February, Maj. Gen. Charles W. Ryder, commanding general of the 34th Division, placed the 1st Battalion, 133rd Infantry at the valley crossroad town Hadjeb El Aioun, located twenty-five miles in front, or east, of a new defensive line at Sbiba Gap. The general told us that we would be the "1st Lost Battalion" of World War II and that we had to hold off the enemy at all costs to allow the division enough time to concentrate on and build a defense at the Sbiba area. What none of us knew at the time was that Rommel had to release his most powerful division, the 10th Panzer Division—probably the most potent and powerful armored division in the world at that time—so it could return to its base east of Fondouk Pass. To reach this base, the 10th Panzer Division had to pass through Hadjeb El Aioun during the early hours of 17 February. Anyone would have predicted that the panzers would smash Company C and the entire 1st Battalion as it rolled through the area.

My first combat mission, as the 1st platoon leader of Company C, was to establish, with my thirty-five men, an outpost on the southeast edge of Hadjeb El Aioun, a position that directly faced the oncoming Germans. Throughout the afternoon of 16 February, we could see the signs—dust clouds made by moving tanks and smoke from burning tanks—that the battle was getting closer—perhaps ten miles away—to our position. We dug in deeper, fully expecting to be attacked the next morning.

Early that night, we received word that we could be relieved if a British force moving from the north arrived at our position by 10:00 p.m. on 16 February 1943.

---

[6] *The 34th Infantry Division.*

[7] *The 1st Infantry Division and the 1st Armored Division.*

As if by magic, two British Bren-gun carriers, commanded by a British major[8], arrived at our position at 10:00 p.m. When I reported to the major, he asked, "Where is the Jerry?"[9]

I told him what we had observed and ventured to say, "The Jerry will be here tomorrow morning."

The major wanted some "petrol," and we happily gave him all that we had. Then he said, "Cheerio!" and rode into the night to do battle.

I told my men to look at that example of valor, noting, "We have just talked to the bravest soldiers we have ever met." I added that if they could be as brave as that little force, we would do well in our future battles.

Our platoon was the rear guard for the battalion as we made a retrograde move of fifteen miles to Kef-El-Ahmar Pass, our next defensive position toward the west. As I recall, most of the men of the battalion rode in trucks, but we walked and had slow going on a rocky, sandy trail. It was comforting to get out of the jam we had been in. And although the enemy had complete local air superiority, we knew that as we walked during the night, we were safe from the enemy's terrorizing air attacks.

17 February

By daylight, we could see the pass about six miles ahead. The mountains on the sides of the pass were 3,000 to 5,000 feet high, while the pass itself lay on the surface level of the relatively flat desert.

Between 8:00 and 9:00 a.m., an astonishing thing was happening in our march. About one-fourth of our men were not keeping up with the rest of us, despite real prodding. In training, this march would have been a piece of cake, but these lag-

---

[8] *While in England in recent years, I read an obituary for a British field-marshall, and it mentioned that as a major he had led his armored force to relieve an American force at Hadjeb El Aioun. When my fellow soldiers and I visited Tunisia in 1995, we found our outpost position, now in town and not at the edge as before, and I was able to verify that we could see for miles to the southeast.*

[9] *What the British called the Germans.*

gards apparently felt the strain of worry, fearing that enemy tanks would overtake us. I halted the unit and called the platoon sergeant, Staff Sgt. Kazebeer, and the platoon guide, Sgt. Holub, both very rugged men. Together the three of us carried the M-1 rifles, two weapons to each of us, of the men who were lagging behind. I also assigned one strong man to each laggard to help move these soldiers along. This process worked—and I learned a valuable lesson: fear can drive some men down mentally and physically and can do so rapidly.

At mid-morning, our platoon entered the very narrow pass, which was wide enough only for a single line of vehicles. Our troops had thrown the personal baggage of our soldiers in the pass to create a makeshift barrier. We did not take the time to search to find our own personal belongings.

Sketch 1

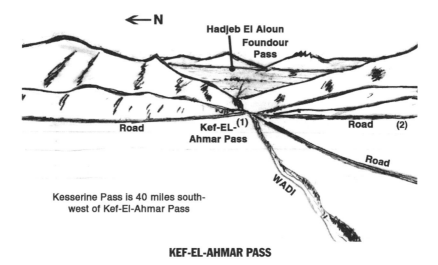

KEF-EL-AHMAR PASS

The 1st Battalion defense was A and B Companies on each shoulder, with C Company in reserve position on a hill at point (1) in Sketch 1. A few French forces straggled through, including a horse-drawn, World War I Howitzer artillery unit, which made it look as if we were fighting in the first World War rather than the second. But French artillery saved the day! Artillery observers joined our men in climbing the shoulders of the pass, and they used flags to adjust the artillery concentrations in mid-afternoon when the German tanks attacked us. The enemy, which we now know consisted of the 10th Panzer Division, was driven back by the French artillery fire.[10]

Toward the end of the day, I received orders to report directly to the battalion commander, Lt. Col. Sheppard. When I reported to him, I was shocked at what I found. He was lying on his back in a one-foot-deep, six-feet-long slit trench. Saluting him was somewhat awkward, but I did so. Using the only map I had seen, he directed me to take his jeep and drive it down the mountain range (see point (2) on Sketch 1) to see if enemy tanks could get through. I looked at the map and remembered the 3,000- to 5,000-foot mountains I had seen as we marched that day. I knew the mountains were similar to the mountains of Virginia, with which I was quite familiar, and I understood the lieutenant colonel's concern, which was a goat trail that wound up and over the mountains near a very tall peak. I refrained from laughing and, instead, had a great jeep ride before assuring him on my return that his flank was secure. He still lay in his trench.

At nightfall, we received orders to move by marching twelve miles back to Hill 620 on the Sbiba defensive line. This position was on the left flank of a tactically perfect, high, two- to three-mile ridge that ran across the Sbiba Gap. It marked the spot where the next battle would be fought.

Rain beat down on us as our platoon led the battalion from the pass area and toward the west. I was not sure I had the right road, so I stopped a jeep coming through with its lights off. I

---

[10] *I should point out, and this is not a complaint, that the 34th Division had not been issued the newest anti-tank weapons, such as the Bazooka. Nor had we received modern radio equipment at the levels of platoon to battalion. One reason for this deficiency was that other U.S. divisions in Tunisia, which had been deployed directly from the United States, brought this equipment with them. Our division, on the other hand, was deployed from Ireland, where modern equipment was not available for issue. In fact, we did not get these items by April.*

stuck my head under the jeep's canvas cover and came face to face with my battalion commander. He almost shouted at me, "Let's get the hell out of here!"

"Very well, sir," I replied and let him splash on. He certainly practiced what he preached: he exited that place in a hurry.

At night, Company C was placed in a battalion reserve position some 300 yards behind the front-line companies. It was a poorly selected position; we had no decent fields of observation to carry out our mission of adding depth to the defense. The ground was so rocky that it was virtually impossible to dig individual slit trenches to provide us with protection against enemy artillery shells. I was quite uncomfortable since I could not see what was going on at the front; nor could we make real plans for any contingency.

But the 34th Division's defense was absolutely superb. Maj. Gen. Ryder had five of his nine infantry battalions, plus three battalions of the 18th Infantry Combat Team[11] and part of the British 1st Guard Brigade. We had possibly as many as four outstanding battalions of division artillery plus access to additional battalions. One hundred fire concentrations were configured to cover the front of three to five miles. Our front-line troops, with their artillery observers, had a grandstand view of the entire battlefield. We were ready, mainly because the 34th Division was together as an infantry-artillery team. The other two U.S. divisions continued to fight as separate regimental combat teams, allowing the Germans to quickly concentrate superior forces against each one, time after time, without having to face massed U.S. artillery fire.

19-24 February

Rommel made his main thrust into the western dorsal area on 19 February, using the 21st Panzer Division to attack the Sbiba Gap. Our heavy artillery fire separated the attacking infantry forces from their tanks, and the Germans made no progress that day at Sbiba Gap. Rommel criticized that first day's action, saying that the attack was not concentrated, that it was

---

[11] *1st Division.*

too spread out.

The day of the 20th, the Germans attempted to sweep around the division's left flank with their tanks. A few broke through the flank, but they had to retreat with some losses. Meanwhile, our position received enemy artillery fire, and Company C lost its first soldier killed in action. He was a company runner, a soldier named Robert Downs. At the time, we were on the division's left flank.

Both the 19th and 20th of February were critical days for decision-making by Rommel. He regained control of the 10th Panzer Division, which started moving on the 19th from Fondouk toward the area to be deployed: either to Sbiba Gap, forty miles from Fondouk, or to Kasserine Pass, eighty miles from Fondouk. The final decision was Kasserine Pass. Rommel must have concluded that the U.S. defense at Sbiba Gap was too much for him to deal with.

The 34th Division had passed its first test in battle. Our troops did not give up a single foot of land to the enemy even though the troops defended a very wide, very vital pass.

At Kasserine, the story was quite different. The very narrow and rugged pass was penetrated thirty miles by 22 February; the Germans turned back on 23 February; and on 24 February, the U.S. forces regained control of Kasserine Pass.

Our platoon went on a night combat patrol to seek contact with the enemy during the night of 21-22 February. We penetrated first about a mile into enemy territory. But the men were making too much noise with their personal equipment, which they had not sound-secured, so I halted and set up an ambush in a dry wadi.[12] I found three men with sound-secured equipment and took them with me two to three miles deeper behind enemy lines. We made no contact at all. Upon our return to the ambush site, I told the men that I expected them to soldier when we fought and if they forgot to soldier, they would go home in a pine box; if they soldiered, they could march back home. We had no more problems with discipline and the men making unnecessary noise.

12 A dry stream bed.

During the night of 22-23 February, the 34th was ordered by higher command to retreat from Sbiba Gap back to Rohia, twelve miles distant. The move was a mistake, so on the morning of 23 February, we were ordered to return to Sbiba Gap. Our battalion was the advance guard for the division, Company C was the advance company, and our 1st platoon was the "point."

As we approached the town of Sbiba, which we had to pass through to reenter our defensive line, I learned from a lone French reconnaissance force that the enemy had advanced to take up positions in the town. The French reported that the Germans had an infantry company and a battery of artillery in the town. At a distance of about two miles from town, I deployed our platoon off the highway and moved directly toward the town over open, sand-dune-covered desert country. I ordered my thirty-five soldiers to spread out in width and depth and to disperse so that each man would occupy an acre of land by himself. Fortunately, farm boys know what an acre of land is! My plan was to advance briskly and, as each man passed over a sand dune to then disappear until he came to the next dune, to fool the enemy into over-counting my strength and conclude that we were a larger force than what we actually were. To my amazement, the rest of the company to my rear did the same thing that we were doing. So to the enemy, we looked like a thousand troops rather than 150 as we advanced.

The enemy force fired a few artillery rounds at us, and we watched in awe as they fled from the town of Sbiba. I learned a valuable lesson right then: you can bluff these Germans.

We returned to our old defensive position on Hill 620. The Battle of Kassserine Pass was over. The Germans began a general movement back to the east on 24 February 1943.

2

Tragedy at Kef-El-Ahmar Pass
Tunisia, 1943

With memories weighing heavily on my heart, I find it difficult to recount the tragic battle that Company C fought to regain control of Kef-El-Ahmar Pass. It was tragic because of leadership mishaps; it was not the fault of the soldiers in the line that brought on the dire misfortune.

After the German forces withdrew from Kasserine Pass on 24 February, they fell back twenty miles to a line at Sbeitla to Hajeb El Aoun. From an outpost fifteen miles west of the town, the Germans guarded Kef-El-Ahmar Pass. The methodical Germans reinforced that outpost each day with a mobile infantry company and four tanks, appearing at 7:00 a.m. each day and remaining throughout the day.

The commander of the 1st Battalion, 133rd Infantry, Lt. Col. Sheppard, received orders to engage the German force at the outpost. I use the term "engage" advisedly since the term actually used is not known. Perhaps it was to "destroy the enemy force" or "move to" or "move onto the pass." My point is that precise orders are very important in battle.

The basic plan for Company C was to advance to the pass area in a daylight move and, under cover of darkness, to proceed to the pass. The remainder of the battalion[1] was kept in reserve and was not committed or placed in a supporting distance to be of any help. I would argue that it was a major error for the battalion to split its forces and not to provide for the larger force[2] to be able to effectively aid and support the smaller force, which was Company C.

Late in the afternoon of 10 March 1943, Company C was hurriedly rushed by truck to a point about four miles from Kef-El-Ahmar Pass. We rapidly left the trucks, which even more rapidly turned around so they could return to the rear. Our 1st Platoon was the advance unit as we moved east on the Sbiba Hajeb El Aoun road. Within a mile, as I advanced beside Lt. Martin Luke,[3] the weapons platoon leader, I spotted two enemy tanks about 600 yards away on a ridge across from the front of us. I yelled to those behind me to hit the ditches, and I hit a ditch quickly myself. Immediately, a tank shell hit the road where I had been walking. Lt. Luke lay in the road under continuous shelling. I thought he was wounded, so I crawled out, under enemy tank fire, and pulled him into my ditch position. Fortunately, he was not wounded, but he was in a state of shock. We suffered no casualties, and we advanced to an assembly area about two miles from the pass, arriving after dark. There we ate a hot supper of oxtail stew, hard crackers, and tea since we were on British rations.

At 10:00 p.m., 1st Lt. Garvin Fitton,[4] the C Company commander, called for me to meet with him and told me to take my platoon to the pass. The night was black and we

[1] *Two infantry companies and a heavy weapons company.*

[2] *The reserve.*

[3] *From Long Island, New York.*

[4] *From Arkansas.*

were in a hollow in the land, so neither of us could even see the pass; nor did we have a map. 1st Lt. Fitton and I tried to determine where the pass was located, and I noticed, barely visible in the skyline, a mountain peak. I suggested that my platoon aim for that peak, which we should reach at 6:00 a.m., and then proceed to the pass, a plan he approved. When I asked if the remainder of the company would maneuver in support, I received no reply. The thought crossed my mind that if the battalion commander wrapped most of his command around him three miles back, maybe the company commander would do the same thing a mile behind our platoon. I dismissed the thought; I had a mission to accomplish. I still thought that since we would be in range of friendly artillery, we would need the support, and only 1st Lt. Fitton could communicate with the artillery.

After the meeting, the platoon moved forward in a single-file formation, with a mortar squad attached, setting a pace at not over one-half mile per hour. We climbed a steep mountain, but I had to go slowly enough that the last group of men—sixty-mm mortar men with heavy ammunition—did not have to run to keep up. I had to ensure that we did not have a break in the line, which would have divided the force.

About an hour later, after we started descending the mountain, we learned that we had an extra mountain ridge in our path. This additional mountain was not visible when we started. In another hour or so, we came upon a second extra mountain ridge that blocked our path. At midnight, I halted the troops and told them that this would be the last break we would take until 6:00 a.m. That grind was necessary in order for us to reach our target.

We climbed and then descended the second extra mountain. I learned that when you're moving at night, it takes just as long to descend a mountain as it does to climb it. At one point, we received word that we had lost a mortar ammunition carrier, the last man in our single-file formation, but we finally did locate him. This situation happened again later that night. Sgt. Holub, who was in control of the men, thought that the missing man had no intention of keeping up with us. But we found him days later; he had been stripped of all clothing, including his shoes, and murdered, probably by rural Arabs.

At 6:00 a.m., just past dawn, we reached our goal, the correct mountain peak, about 1,000 yards from the pass. The ridge reminded me of a dinosaur's tail. At 6:30 a.m., after we had eaten, we prepared to move out toward the pass and began rapidly descending the grade of three to one—or thirty-three percent—by moving squads from peak top to peak top.

Looking to the east across the desert, as the day began to get brighter, we spotted four enemy tanks and three enemy trucks five miles away and rapidly approaching the pass. Each truck carried at least twenty-five German soldiers. The enemy would reach the pass much sooner than we could—and we were outnumbered. The lower we went toward the pass, the easier it would become for the enemy to take the high ground behind us and cut us off. By then, the remainder of our company was out of sight—and we had good observation in every direction.

We advanced two squads forward to two peak tops about 600 to 800 yards from the pass and set up the single mortar to fire on the enemy troops in the trucks when they came within range of 1,600 yards.

At 7:00 a.m., the tanks drove through the pass. The infantrymen in the trucks were standing. The trucks parked closely together next to the pass, presenting a perfect mortar target! When we directed the mortar to fire from the forward, or enemy, side of the slope, we had a bit of a delay because the mortar sergeant wanted to be conventional, which meant he did not want to be on that forward slope. However he moved to the forward slope and gave the order for the first round to be fired. It landed so far from the target that it took a minute or two for us to see the explosion of dust when it rose from a distant canyon. We missed the mark so badly that the enemy never even saw it. The second round of fire was still too deep, missing the target by at least 400 yards. The German infantry was still in the trucks, so, hoping for luck, I told the sergeant to bring the mortar fire in 400 yards and to fire all of his rounds. Again we missed. But this time, the Germans left their trucks and disappeared. Since we had no communication with our accompanying observer, who was with the other part of our company, we could not call for artillery.

We kept sharp eyes on where the German infantry company was located. Surprise! In about two hours, the Germans, in close marching order—a company drill formation—moved through the pass and suddenly halted on a flat, open, and dry riverbed. The enemy soldiers did a left face, standing in formation about 1,000 yards from us. We got all of our men to put their battle sights on their M-1 rifles—at maximum range—and looked for the remainder of C Company to ensure that we would not spray them with "friendly fire."

Again, to our surprise, we saw the C Company men deployed in a line on a very, very small hill by the dry river bed—and only 200 yards from the enemy! What a perfect ambush! I told my men to hold their fire until they saw C Company fire first. My idea was to let the company completely surprise the enemy. We did not want to interfere with their battle, but we were prepared to support their expected effort. Their eighty riflemen at 200-yard range would be much more effective than my thirty-five men would have been at 1,000-yard range.

But C Company never fired on the enemy. In later years, man after man, including survivors and POWS, told me— and others—that the order to fire was never given. Sergeants have told me that they pleaded with the commander to let them fire their machine guns and semi-automatic rifles. Without a doubt, the entire enemy company would have been destroyed in less than a minute with rifle fire alone. But after about fifteen minutes of standing in the dry riverbed as perfect targets, the Germans returned to the pass. No one had taken a single shot at them during that time! We had our own artillery observer; why we failed to use our artillery is puzzling! At that point, an Arab on a white horse circled C Company. As he returned to the pass area, our platoon fired on him. The Arab had gone on a reconnaissance for the Germans and noted that the company was concentrated on a small hill. We fired on him hoping that the Germans would think we were a large force coming to the aid of C Company. The enemy tanks moved to roads, about three miles from us and drove off a U.S. light tank force.

At approximately 2:00 p.m., the German infantry made a swift, very professional flank assault on C Company's right flank, moving through the forward two platoons and the two machine guns. We could not fire on the Germans because they were suddenly in the midst of the company's positions and firing would have endangered our own men. The enemy achieved success in a matter of minutes, loading our men as prisoners of war into trucks. The trucks and tanks pulled away to head east. Again, we could not fire on them for fear of hurting our own troops. About seventy U.S. soldiers were killed in action, wounded in action, or taken prisoners. Most of these losses were from C Company.

The aftermath of this tragedy was that the battalion commander was reduced in rank and sent to the rear. Since the company commander was taken prisoner, 1st Lt. Earl C. Moses,[5] a VMI graduate who was considered the best lieutenant in the regiment, was chosen to be the new company commander and had the first choice of any of the officers in the regiment for assignment to the company. We received new replacements.

My platoon suffered no losses; nor did most of the company headquarters, except for the commander and the first sergeant, Roy Larkin, both of whom were captured by the

[5] *From Kansas.*

Germans. My platoon sergeant, Kazebeer, became the new first sergeant. The weapons platoon had lost about half of its men, and the other two rifle platoons were mostly lost. After that debacle, we trained. We patrolled against the enemy around Sbeitla, and in about a month we were once again ready for action. But we felt the loss of our men very deeply.[6]

---

[6] *In our 1995 visit to Tunisia, we spent more time at this battle site than at any other site. We spent one afternoon on the east side, the next half day on the west side. We saw where all the positions were, where the Company C command post was, and where the enemy could have been completely destroyed. And we wondered why the order to fire never came. Bob Woodford said he was with our platoon in our high ground positions; Wes Gallup was with the weapons platoon in the main company positions. As we compared our recollections, we envisioned the battle again—and we were in agony. Robert Wessels, who was a POW of the Germans, said that the German force at this battle was part of the 96th Light Infantry Brigade. They were fortunate—we were not.*

The Battle for Fondouk Pass
Tunisia, 1943

Fondouk Pass, in north central Tunisia, was a stronghold area for the German forces in early April 1943. It was vital to the Germans that the pass be held because if the Allies breached it, they would cut the supply line to German forces who were in the south battling the advance of the British 8th Army under Montgomery.

An Allied attack from west to east was launched by a British-American combined force commanded by a Britisher. British forces were to seize the left (north) pass shoulder, while American forces were to seize the right shoulder. Once the shoulders were seized, British tanks would sally forth toward the coast and cut off the German forces.

The 34th Division of the American forces attacked with three regiments abreast. The 135th Infantry, 133rd Infantry, and the 168th Infantry were in line from north to south on a two-mile front, crossing a valley some ten miles wide. The desert area during that time of the year was green with springtime growth, mainly poppies in full bloom with long stems stretching up two or more feet from the ground. The area for which we were responsible was very gentle and rolling slightly down in the center, then rising slightly toward the base of the mountains. The highest mountain in the range was the objective of the 133rd Infantry Regiment. Designated as Hill 306, the mountain was about 1,000 feet high.

Although the coordinated attack by all forces began on 8 April 1943, that day was filled with changes. Friendly air attacks were scheduled, canceled, and then rescheduled, only to be re-canceled. The Allied forces made no progress. It was a bad omen. The only airplanes we saw were about forty flights of German Stuka planes that attacked us and our forces.

On 9 April, our platoon was in the assault wave on the left of Company C, its two platoons of infantrymen up front. We had two squads forward and one to the rear in staggered column formations, with much dispersion in depth and width between all men. I led our troops. At about 5,000 yards from our mountain objective, and early in the day, we advanced and all was in order. It appeared to me that all troops to my left and right were up on line, as far as I could see, for about a mile in each direction. It was the only time in my life I could witness three regiments at one time on a battlefield, and it was a thrilling site to behold.

As we all crossed a wide, shallow, dry wadi, I received an "order"—like a direct order from Above—to save my men by directing them to "hit the dirt." This premonition hit me as real and forceful. It was instantaneous, and I acted swiftly without hesitation. I waved and yelled for the men to go down, which they did promptly. Across and up and down our advancing front line of troops, a huge, laterally concentrated volley of incoming German artillery shells burst in and on us when all of the men—except for mine—were walking upright. Following the barrage of shells, I heard many screams from the wounded to my left and right. When a pause came in the enemy firing, I rushed my men forward, and, once again, I received that "word." Again I got my men down and again we received volleys of enemy artillery fire. With another pause in the firing, I once more rushed all of us forward and onward. We did not lose a single man; however, the men in other units around us suffered many casualties, some severe.

Then we moved aggressively forward. By then, I could not

see any of our troops to my left or right. We were "spearheading" the attack—and we were all alone.

As we came closer to the mountain objective, which was less than 2,000 yards away, we began to receive long-range enemy machine-gun fire. I had each squad leader move his men forward one man at a time, with each man running forward ten to twenty yards, then hitting the ground. We all advanced that way. Often, machine-gun bullets cut the long poppy stems surrounding our prone bodies as we hugged the ground. We moved onward steadily—but strongly—in spite of this enemy fire.

I halted the attack when I received a verbal message, relayed voice-to-voice by men behind me, to report back to a colonel. I went back in small rushes the same way we had advanced. The enemy tried to shoot me but kept missing at that long range. I found Lt. Col. Carley L. Marshall, to whom I was to report. Lt. Col. Marshall lay prone on the ground, and I bounced into a face-to-face ground landing, saluting and reporting at the same time to the new battalion commander. He said that I was now the new Company C commander since Lt. Moses was wounded. He ordered me to move my troops forward to a large cactus patch, which we could both see near the base of the mountain, where I would receive further instructions. We exchanged some short, pleasant conversation and learned that we were both native Virginians and had the same heroes: J.E.B. Stuart and Gen. Robert E. Lee. He told me that he had been a 2nd lieutenant for eighteen years; I had been one for less than a year.

After returning to my men, we closed onto the cactus patch, which we reached late that afternoon. We received enemy fire all the way, but all thirty-six men were accounted for. I spent the remaining daylight hours going back to round up other men. I found twenty-one and brought them forward to join our thirty-six.

After dark, I assembled with the other four company commanders at the 1st Battalion's forward command post. Lt. Col. Marshall opened the meeting by saying that Gen. Robert E. Lee always had a council of war with his corps commanders. I was the lone company commander who knew exactly what he meant and was ready when he asked me, "What shall we do?"

I pointed to the mountain and said, "Sir, there are three prominent peaks. Give Company C the tallest peak in the center and we will take it. Give A and B Companies the other two peaks in a simultaneous attack. Sir, we should attack when the moon wanes."[1]

Lt. Col. Marshall ordered Company C to take the tall peak in the center, another company to take the left peak, and another company to remain in reserve. We would attack when the moon waned. I really was not too amazed that he took my suggestions on how to attack but was somewhat disappointed that he did not include the right flank peak. As a result, we had to worry about our right side, especially in defending our peak after we took it.

Later, after we advanced about 600 yards from the base of the mountain, I made a personal reconnaissance forward for about 400 yards. The land was gentle, sandy, non-vegetative, and sloped slightly to the base of the mountain. I was very quiet and listening intensely, and I heard a little tinkling of metal up and down the base of the mountain. I concluded that the Germans had at least four machine guns there, all set up to provide the enemy with interlocking fields of grazing fire, giving the Germans almost perfect bands of grazing defensive machine-gun fire across the whole front. I was so close to the Germans that I could smell the food they were eating. I knew where they were and believed that possibly later they would go to sleep and we could surprise them by stealth. Germans did not like to fight at night; night was my favorite time to attack.

My scheme of attack was to use stealth, as long as we could, and to attack with all fifty-seven men on a line, with the men prepared to use assault rifle fire only if the enemy fired at us first.

About 500 yards from the base of the mountain, I dug, with my boot, a long line parallel to the mountain. The line was

---

[1] *It was then about 8:00 p.m. The near new moon would disappear at about 10:30 p.m. In those days, all country boys knew that.*

about 200 yards in length. All fifty-seven men moved to that line, and I ensured that the non-commissioned officers were dispersed evenly for maximum control. We did not have any other officers with our force.

While waiting for the moon to wane, I went to each man and whispered for him to point his rifle to the center peak—our objective. To each I gave a word or two of encouragement about where the enemy was and how we would get past that enemy at the mountain base. We had complete silence discipline. After I settled in the center of the line to get some rest, I heard a booming voice way down on the right flank that shattered our silence. As I recall, it said, "Lieutenant, this is Pvt. Hempstead. When you tell us there ain't no Germans upon that mountain, you are a damn liar, but I will tell you what we will do! We will get on top of that mountain and brew tea on the backs of dead Germans!"

The men chuckled all up and down the line. I walked in front of the troops and moved toward Pvt. Hempstead. Despite the fact that I had told all the men that the enemy was on the mountain, I had the feeling that Hempstead had done more for morale than I had. Finding Pvt. Hempstead, I ordered him to stand up. He did and saluted. In a loud voice I said, "Pvt. Hempstead, you are now a sergeant in the U.S. Army. Take command of the three men to your right[2] and protect our right flank."

"Very well, sir," he replied.

I turned to all of the men and said, "Let's go!"

The moon had almost waned. We could see men up and down the line, perhaps twenty or more. They formed a straight line, like a parade formation but hunkered down in a slouching position, quiet, alert, ready, and moving forward.

At the base of the mountain, all of us were still on line. We moved quickly, but quietly, up the slopes of the mountain, which was perfectly smooth for walking and had a gradual upgrade. No one broke stride. Part way up the grade, someone—friend or foe—dropped a piece of metal, and it tinkled down

[2] *Our flank.*

the slope. We froze in place. Suddenly, four enemy machine guns opened up with deadly firing—but all of the guns were behind us and were firing over the area from which we had advanced. I ordered the squad sergeants to throw grenades down onto the firing guns, which quickly silenced them one by one. Then we swiftly moved forward and up, each man in a race with the others to reach the top of the mountain.

A quick reconnaissance showed me that the back—or east—side of the mountain was a steep escarpment, so there was little chance for a counter-attack from that direction. I told the men to turn around and face west, the way from which we had advanced, and to set up a defensive line. I gave the new Sgt. Hempstead more men and told him to guard what was now our left flank, which was exposed to the enemy.

All night long, we conducted a series of small, uncoordinated counter-attacks. The password was "grocery store." Often during the night, we were comforted by Sgt. Hempstead bellowing out, "Grocery, you SOB, you don't know store," and then cutting loose at his target, an attacking German soldier or soldiers, with his trusty M-1 rifle.

At daybreak, some seventy dead Germans lay in front of us. We could see the sea some forty to fifty miles to the east, and we could also see German forces fleeing—with our artillery fire making them flee even faster.

Our 1st Battalion was the only 34th Division infantry battalion to take any mountain in this division attack. We took Hill 306 that night of 9 and 10 April 1943 and were given a new name: The Break-through Battalion.

An interesting note is that the official history of the U.S. Army in MTO includes a map with a postscript that at 8:00 p.m. on 9 April 1943, Hill 306 was still in German hands. That's true, but at 11:00 p.m., I can assure you, it was in the hands of the U.S. soldiers of Company C of the 133rd Infantry.

In working on this history, I found in my files a letter (see page 29) to my parents that I had typed after the Battle of Fondouk Pass. It was dated 25 April 1943. The "Margaret" in the letter, in 1945, became my wife and companion and later the mother of our four wonderful children. "Press" is my sole brother. He flew B-17 missions from England to Germany in 1945. He survived the war and became a successful business-man and had an outstanding family. He also has four wonder-ful children. "Mr. Meanley," who died in the early 1950s, was my oldest friend in my hometown. When I was young, he was my hero.

I like my comment about my mother: "I can see her now [sic] she would understand more than anyone else." My moth-er took me to the Gettysburg Battlefield for two consecutive summers, probably in 1932 and 1933. While there, we always stayed within the Confederate lines. I repeatedly re-enacted Pickett's charge with his Virginia troops and obeyed my mother when she told me, over and over, to "take Little Round Top Mountain—get there before the Yankees get there." Even as a child, I had already been taught by my mother how to take mountaintops!

April 25, 1943

Dear Mother and Father,

Here I am pecking away again. I wish I could hear from someone back home but we have had no mail for ages. Also it is no use of ever trying to get that radio tube for me. I put the radio in my barracks bag to store for me but someone decided that they should be salvaged so it is gone. I felt for all my men they had all their personal possessions in theirs. That was all I lost almost. Its very nice here every morning early birds with the most beautiful voiced awaken me. I love the re-sponsibility I now have. It is awful amount of work to it but I get results. Besides I don't have the time to think of the ones back home which I certainly love to do, but I realize that this is my mission now so my next mission will be at home. My new Colonel is a Virginia man and believe me he is certainly a great help not that he does it himself but he is a old timmer and I listen to the sound principles that he works on. I have learned plenty from him, especially exactness of de-tails and much about men and how to deal with them. All of these things give me confidence in myself. Here I am talking all about myself so you see I must be down to the last resort; but after all one cannot mention much mostly because we do nothing or see anything that can be mentioned.

I will put into this letter something that is very dear to me be-cause it was written by my men about me. Certainly I am not "Cocky" about it because when one does his duty as he sees fit it is stored only in one small portion of my mind. What I do think of is the devotion of the men whom I lead. I wished my Father could have seen it, it was an inspiration to see such men unhestitatedly go forward. I thought of Mr. Meanley. I know he would approve and by all means show him this letter. I thought of Margaret and knew she sould be proud and Mother I can see her now she would understand more than anyone else. I thought of Press, Tom and Peyton they would have done the same as I. So you see it was really nothing to it. Here it goes I know that you know the spirit that it is being sent to you. "In late afternoon and early evening of 1943 in vicinity of Blank Pass Tunisia. During the afternoon the Company Commander was wounded while leading his company. Lt. Wilkinson took command of the company and other units and continued the attack. Going from group to group Lt. Wilkinson rallied his men for an attack on the strong enemy positions despite heavy long range machine gun fire. At a late hour that night Lt. Wilkinson lead his company up a very steep and rocky mountain to take the enemy positions. Heavy resistance was met but was quickly overcome after the positions were taken etc. Lt. Wilkinson' bravery under fire and excellent leadership is a credit to the armed forces of the United States of America.

For goodness sakes do not show this to those who do not understand. My citation and medal will be quite nice.

Write Press that I think of him often and will enjoy hearing of his experiences. I hope that we can finish this mess before he and the rest of the boys have to come.

I hope you both are well. I am enjoying excellant health and am fine. Have quite a longing for home again but surely I will be so happy when I come back. In all the world there is no place like our America.

Love, Richard

4

The Pool Table
Near Alife, Italy, 1943

In 1943, the 34th Division made the first crossing of the Volturno River on 13 October, made a second crossing on 18 October, and made a third crossing on 3 November. This is the story of Company C during the second crossing.

The Volturno River snaked back and forth through mountain valleys in Italy in the general area between Naples and Rome. Because of this twisting, the division had to cross the river three times since it was always attacking to the north.

The 1st Battalion attempted to cross the river on 18 October but simply got lost.

The German force defending our crossing was the 29th Panzer Grenadier Regiment of the 3rd Panzer Division, one of the best German forces in Italy at that time. The Germans skillfully selected the most narrow part of the mountain valley to establish a strong defensive line between two valley villages, Dragoni and Alife, which hugged the sides of opposing mountains. A road and a railroad, which connected the towns, crossed the Volturno River, located midway between both towns, via a bridge.

The mission of the 133rd Infantry Regiment was to cross the river, move upstream along the bank, seize the bridge, and then attack the enemy along the defensive line established between Dragoni and Alife. The 1st Battalion was to cross the river and seize the bridge. The 100th Battalion, a Japanese-American/American unit, was to continue through the 1st Battalion and attack the German defensive line. The 3rd Battalion did not have to cross the river but was to attack the enemy defensive line between Dragoni and the river bank.

My role was that of platoon leader of the 1st Platoon of Company C. On 18 October, I patrolled with PFC Enrico Caruso of Cleveland, Ohio. We crossed the river, turned left, and went upstream toward the bridge. We moved carefully, using trees and other vegetation near the bank for concealment. Gradually, the bridge came into sight 100 yards away—and we saw a German sentry. We spotted a low manmade waterfall about sixty yards from the bridge, so we crawled in the tall grass to the waterfall. There, we determined that we could move across the river and remain hidden from sight from the German soldier on the bridge. Although we walked under the falling water, we did not get too wet. Crossing the river, we

Sketch 2

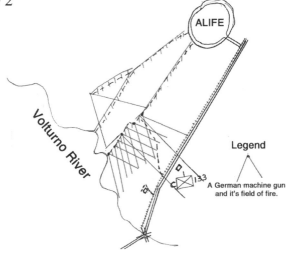

POOL TABLE, 20 OCTOBER 1943

went about two miles to the Dragoni area to make contact with our 3rd Battalion. After an exchange of information, we returned by the same route.

Under darkness on 19 October, the battalion crossed the river,[1] and lead elements moved slowly toward the bridge. However, the Germans blew up the bridge before we were able to take it.

Before daylight on 20 October and in a heavy fog, the 100th Battalion began to attack the Dragoni-Alife defensive line about 500 yards from the riverbank. The Germans had selected a very flat area with many small, pastured, and closely grazed fields surrounded by numerous hedgerows as their "killing zone." The 100th Battalion was turned back by daylight.

The 1st Battalion was ordered to attack through the 100th Battalion and to seize the enemy defensive line in a frontal assault. Capt. Moses, who had resumed command of Company C, took the officers who would lead the assault forward to reconnoiter and to issue attack orders.

As we passed through some elements of the 100th Battalion, I noticed that some of the men were huddled closely together, and I wanted to go over and order them to disperse and spread out. One enemy shell could have killed twenty to thirty of them, and I wanted to save them from that fate. If it had been my command, I would not have hesitated to issue such an order, but I could not make myself do that to troops that I did not command. Besides, they were frantically digging individual slit trenches for protection. In a few cases during the frenzy, some soldiers threw dirt out so fast that some of it was going into the trench that another soldier was digging.[2]

We went forward beyond the 100th Battalion's positions to view the new battlefield as best we could in the fog. We saw in the flat, even, closely grazed grass many long streaks where enemy machine guns had fired and bullets had skirted along the even surface, proof of the intensity of the close enemy firing

---

[1] *I have no recollection of that event.*

[2] *In explanation, the 100th Battalion was a new, green unit. In the future, I always saw them execute their affairs in an excellent manner.*

guns. The crisscrossing paths of streaks in the grass indicated that that area was a potential death trap to anyone trying an assault across that stretch of land. This area was known as the "Pool Table."

Capt. Moses had a zone to attack and ordered a frontal attack. I asked for a moving artillery barrage across our front, fire power that we could "lean into" and use to overcome the enemy positions. The captain requested the artillery support but was told that close-in firing support could not be registered and observed for control due to the heavy fog, so the request was denied. I asked for permission to maneuver my platoon to the left, across our front, for about 400 yards to the river, then to turn up the river and strike the enemy on his exposed flank. That request was approved.

I returned to my troops and told them of my attack plan. I also told them not to verbally comment to any 100th Battalion soldier when we passed through their positions. I knew that soldiers normally cursed out loud if they had to accomplish a mission that another unit had failed to fulfill.

The fog was so thick that it was difficult to see a man five yards away. The formation was two squads up and one behind. I was forward and between the two squad leaders. Caruso, the radioman, was five yards behind me. Each of the two forward squad leaders was five yards to each side of Caruso, and the remaining men were five yards apart.

We moved silently and slowly, hoping the enemy would not hear us. We were exposed and vulnerable but only if the Germans detected our movement and began firing their weapons. I had reason to believe that the enemy was no closer than 100 yards and probably even as far away as 200 yards. We moved for about 400 yards toward the river, always parallel to the enemy's front line.

I turned our formation to the right and aimed for the enemy's flank, wherever that was in the heavy fog! A few minutes later, I unexpectedly spotted the end of a German machine-gun barrel right in front of me at a distance of five yards. I dove directly under the barrel and grabbed for my single grenade.

Pool Table Battlefield. Germans held defensive positions in the hedgerows.

The German gunner began firing—and I was under the barrel of his gun! Obviously, he didn't know my location. I tossed the grenade a short distance. Luckily, the German was firing from an ancient sunken farm-road, so the shrapnel from the grenade hit him and missed me. My grenade silenced the gun. With one other man, I moved up the sunken road and found another gun that had been abandoned. Other than the man with me, I could not see any of my men because of the fog.

At midmorning the fog lifted, and we spotted a German tank approaching us at a rather fast rate of speed. Since we were exposed to the tank, we went to some heavy trees near the river for protection. Eventually, I was able to gather together about half of my platoon. The enemy tank withdrew, and we returned to the area that we had previously penetrated.

This attack—and others—broke through the enemy's defensive line. The Germans withdrew during the day to set up other new defenses for our forces to attack on another day.[3]

---

[3] *In our visit to the Pool Table in 1984, we walked and drove all over the battlefield, seeing it in much detail. I recalled, then, that in 1944, I took Company C twice to walk through the battlefield as a training exercise. I had the survivors of the 1943 battle tell the story of what happened on 20 October1943 to the new replacements.*

Eldon Johnson and Everett "Corney" Cornelius examine military maps at the Pool Table in 1984.

Volturno River

C Company Battle for Hill 550: Third Crossing of the Volturno River
Italy, 1943

The control of Hill 550, a mountain nearly 1,800 feet high in the center of a regimental zone of attack, was vital, and the fight for control of it became an epic battle for Company C, 133rd Regiment. The mountain marked the beginning of the defensive "Winter Line" of the German forces; it also controlled the valley to the south. If the Germans held Hill 550, our artillery and engineer forces would not be able to enter the valley to provide the necessary support to the infantry. If our infantry forces could seize Hill 550, we could begin to penetrate the German Winter Line. The defensive area extended twenty to thirty miles to Cassino to the north, through formidable mountains whose bare tops extended above the treeline.

This battle was a 133rd Infantry Regiment battle. Col. Carley L. Marshall, the commander, artfully designed a bold night attack by secretly assembling most of the regiment and moving the men swiftly across the Volturno River, through the valley, and onto the mountains two to three miles away. His success depended on passing enemy outpost lines in the valley and arriving on top of the mountains by daylight. Moving at night avoided the costly field-by-field attacks under intense enemy artillery fire that a daylight attack would have precipitated. Only a very disciplined and highly trained infantry could execute such a plan.

Sketch 3

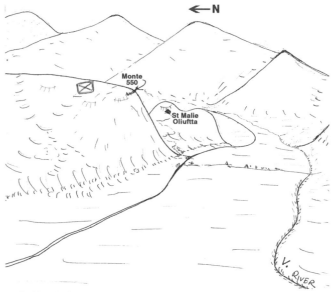

THIRD CROSSING OF VOLTURNO RIVER, 3-11 NOVEMBER 1943

The nighttime assembly of the regiment at the edge of the Volturno River was professionally executed by the infantry companies coming out of the mountains to the south and arriving on schedule to cross the river at 10:00 p.m. The water, which was about three or four feet deep, was cold, and the current was almost strong enough to knock a man over if he tripped over the rocks hidden beneath the surface.

The objective of the 1st Battalion, under Lt. Col. Eugene Moseley, was Hill 550. Company C was the left assault company. The 3rd Battalion was to veer to the right and seize St. Marie Olivetto, a mountain village at a low altitude. The 100th Battalion initially followed the 1st Battalion and then veered to the left to take smaller hills lying to the left of Hill 550. First Lt.

Martin Luke, infantry, from Jamaica, New York,[1] was the company commander. A first lieutenant of infantry from Toano, Va., I was the executive officer and second in command.

Silent, swift, single-file column movements carried the company through the German outpost line. Factors in our favor were our quiet movements, our boldness, and the tendency of the Germans to relax at night when they did not expect U.S. forces to attack.

By early light the next morning, the lead platoons had reached the base of Hill 550 and were ready to climb the mountain. Chances were good that we could reach the top of Hill 550 before the enemy knew we had arrived since the Germans had no view of our troops as we climbed.

At about 7:00 a.m., two German Messerschmidt-109 jet planes attacked Company C near the junction where our column was crossing the main valley highway. The planes appeared suddenly from the north or northeast, flying very low and firing guns across our column. I ordered company headquarters troops to "hit the ditches"; then I ordered PFC Everett "Corny" Cornelius from Houston, Texas, to fire his rifle at the two planes just crossing to our front. At a range less than 150 yards, he fired at the closest plane. Cornelius said, "I led them like shooting ducks. I could see the side of the pilot's head." He probably shot the German pilot in the head. The plane never lifted from its parallel flight pattern next to the ground; it veered to its right and crashed into the German-held mountains to our west. Cornelius implied that there was nothing to it, but I can tell you that it was "tall Texas" shooting![2]

By approximately 8:00 a.m., the headquarters group arrived at the base of the mountains. Soon thereafter, I received word by radio to report to the forward company command post, which was a short distance up the side of the mountain. Arriving there, I found Lt. Luke with a shrapnel wound to the head, but he was conscious and talking. He wanted to carry on

[1] *Long Island*

[2] *I personally regret that a medal of valor was not presented to PFC Cornelius, who deserves to be honored in some fashion.*

as the commander of the company but soon became less able to talk. Although I hated to see him go, I decided that he had to be evacuated. We were as close as junior officers in combat can be and loved talking together. He was a sophisticated New Yorker, a commercial artist in peacetime, and fully devoted to being a good professional infantry officer in wartime. He liked to tell me about his life and enjoyed tales of my life, which contrasted to his Jewish, "city" background. My upbringing as an eastern Virginia country boy, educated in conservation and forestry at Virginia Polytechnic Institute,[3] which was then a military college, fascinated him because it was such a different beginning in life compared to his own. I felt the same way about him.

I assumed command of Company C and ordered 1st Sgt. Patrick, a burly, combative, young Irish-American from the original cadre of the unit, to establish a rear command post site at the mountain base. I received word that our troops on the left of Hill 550 had possibly been turned back by the enemy and that the troops on the right could possibly be on top of Hill 550. Since the top of the hill was most important to me, we moved first to that area. My forward command post group was small. It consisted of Corny Cornelius, a radioman, and me. As it turned out, this group became not only the command group, but also part of the firing line infantry group for the duration of this battle, which lasted for several days.

Before 10:00 o'clock that morning, we arrived near the top and joined a small, disorganized group of about twenty-five troops. I moved them swiftly to the very top and into the very position that the Germans had dug to defend the mountain. We had a real advantage; we had beaten the Germans and had taken the battle positions from them without a fight.

To me, our first priority was to hold the new line. Most certainly, the enemy would fight to recover it since the line had the best areas for observation. If it were taken from us, the enemy could bring artillery fire on all of our future movements of our

[3] *Virginia Polytechnic Institute, popularly called VPI when I studied there, is now Virginia Polytechnic Institute and State University, popularly called Virginia Tech today.*

own artillery and on our engineer bridge, where our units were crossing the river to our rear.

My reconnaissance of the area began after I had organized the fields of fire for the troops. The first surprise of the terrain features was that the top of the mountain was relatively flat, with a few boulders here and there, along with some low trees and bushes. The flatness extended for varied distances of about 100 to 150 yards to what appeared to be a stonewall that ran parallel to our front lines. I was tempted to move to that wall line, but with my small force, I knew the enemy could get behind it and surround us. We could now defend both the forward and the rear approaches of our troops. The wall did not appear to me to have any more observation advantages than what we already had.[4] Another reason that I did not move to the wall was that our defensive line could provide a flat killing zone for our riflemen against a frontal counterattack.

Word came that the left company troops had secured positions and that an officer was in charge. No other officers were with me. We heard our battalion troops occasionally firing to our right, some 200 to 300 yards downhill from us. We did not make contact with them since we needed every man to hold our line. I had a mixture of men from two rifle platoons and a few sergeants. Our three 60-mm mortars were in support; our two machine guns were on the company's left flank and remained there during the battle.

For the next six days, we held our line against very heavy enemy howitzer-artillery fire and continual blasts of machine-gun fire, which we immediately returned with our own Browning automatic rifle (BAR) and M-1 rifle fire. We could silence the machine-gun fire, but the artillery fire was devastating. My attrition rate of wounded was two or three a day, on average, so my small force was reduced to squad-size during this period. After the battle ended, I counted about 3,000 new shell holes

---

[4] *In 1984, Corny and I climbed to the top of Hill 550. The stonewall was still there; in fact, nothing had changed. Even the positions the Germans had dug and where we fought from remained intact. We verified that the stonewall position would have given us no advantages for observation.*

down in the valley below, which was behind us and near the base of the mountain. I estimated that one of every three enemy shells hit our position on the mountaintop. The near misses of screaming shells tore past us about 100 feet in the air and then plunged to the valley below. We actually saw the rear of the enemy shells in flight!

The Germans wanted to take our position very badly, but our rifle firepower never allowed them to mount an assault. We had accumulated eight BARs to give us maximum firepower, so we kept cracking bullets over the stonewall to show the enemy that we intended to hold our position. At the end—the sixth day—we caught more glimpses of Germans near the wall area and experienced an increase in enemy machine-gun fire. I surmised that they would counterattack the next morning.

That night, I got 1st Sgt. Patrick to send up extra blank magazines for the BARs, along with extra 30-caliber rifle ammunition. We filled the new magazines with ammunition. Each of the eight men we had left knew the planned action for the next morning. We would all rapid-fire our weapons in mass to get the Germans to think that we had been reinforced and would attack them. Ruses sometimes work!

Early the next morning, at my command, we began our mass rifle-firing. After about a minute or two, a white flag rose from behind the enemy stonewall. Down the line, a second, then a third flag went up. We were amazed! Was the ruse really working?

Ordering "Cease fire!" and telling the men to be ready to return fire only on my orders, I shouted in English for the Germans to "stand up on the wall!" We saw, in astonishment, about fifty German soldiers wearing helmets and boots, but carrying no visible weapons, jump onto the wall and stand there. I then ordered, "Jump down in front and halt!" And they did. They stood about 100 yards from us. Then I ordered, "March forward in line!" They came toward us in a straight line and in a quick step. When they were about forty yards away, a German order barked out that we didn't understand. All of the Germans then reached toward their boots to grab stick-grenades, which had been placed in the boot-tops. Quickly I gave the order "Commence firing!" Our volley was devastating. All of the Germans fell, resembling 100-pound sacks of potatoes being kicked over. No enemy grenades were ever thrown at us since they never had a chance.

We rushed forward to capture about thirty who had not been casualties. A German sergeant was down and badly wounded in the leg. He looked up at me and said in clear English, "Lieutenant, I am wounded; I need help."

"Order your men to help you off the battlefield," I replied.

"My men will not obey my orders now," he said.

"Very well," I responded, and I ordered two German soldiers to carry him off the field. Most of the enemy soldiers said they were Austrians. Who knows if that were true? The army sergeant, on the other hand, must have been German and could very well have been dropped and abandoned by the two soldiers when they were out of our sight.

This bloody battle was over.[5] We had seized and held the most critical mountain in the regimental sector. Hill 550 was ours!

Postscript

In 1984, Corny Cornelius and I climbed Hill 550 to this battle spot. The site was vivid in my memory since we had spent eight days there in 1943. In all of the years since the battle, the site had not changed. Resting there, after spending hours looking at the area from the German viewpoints and from the area where American heroes had fought so gallantly, Corny said to me," And we thought right after the victory, that you had gone off your rocker when you told us to clean up the battlefield and hide all the shiny tin ration cans in a cave down below us." I asked where the cave was, and with his keen memory for details of terrain, he replied, "Right down there." We both ran to

---

[5] *Sgt. Eldon Johnson recalls that when we moved forward through the German-held area, he saw more bloody bandages on the ground than he had ever seen before.*

the spot he had remembered and removed some rock and soil to find piles of rusty ration cans—which we both still have. We also have many photographs of this battle area.

My memory then came complete circle. This battle had begun with an air attack, and I wanted those cans hidden so they would not attract enemy planes and initiate another attack against us. We had had enough!

Without my knowledge, 1st Sgt. Patrick had submitted a Citation of Gallantry for me. I was as surprised as anyone could be when Gen. Clark, commanding general of the 5th Army in Italy, pinned the Silver Star on my battle jacket a bit later. In a true sense, the valor and gallantry belonged to those members of Company C, 133rd Infantry Regiment, whose actions I have tried to record in these pages. Unfortunately, I can no longer recall the names of most of these soldiers.

Winter Warfare
on the Way to Cassino
Italy, 1944

By mid-December 1943, Company C had settled down in an olive orchard in the Piedmont d'Alife area, well behind the front lines. The general silence of the area was comforting; the aged olive trees in the orchard seemed to add to the sense of security as our olive-drab pyramid squad tents blended in with the winter colors of the leaves of the trees.

The men had bounced back. The cold and wetness of the past frontline positions were gone, leaving both body and soul restored.

The olive orchard was on the family farm of Samuel Lumbar. He and his family lived there in a stone farmhouse nestled in the orchard. Company C headquarters, supply, and kitchen were approximately 200 feet in front of the home. The rifle and weapons platoons were given areas surrounding the home, which sat in the center of the farm.

Samuel "Sam" Lumbar was a wiry man, about fifty years old, and his heavier wife was the mother of several children. As the father, Sam was a good provider. He was quiet, his wife was cheerful, and the children were well behaved. We liked the family and all of us helped Sam with his tasks.

At night, the big center room of the house served as a social center. Some of us would meet there, drink wine, eat fresh black-bread and country cheese, and talk. The room had a fireplace, but no electricity, so it was a simple gathering spot for comradeship under what seemed to us rather ancient and quaint conditions. At the close of our first meeting in the center room, Sam and his wife insisted, in Italian, that I stay in their home. I was led up the outside steps to an upstairs bedroom at the end of the stairs. The mattress on the bed was filled with dried cornhusks and the blankets were heavy wool; I slept soundly each night. I knew that at daybreak each day, I would find all of my clothes washed and dried; even my trench coat was ironed and my boots cleaned.

We were allowed to establish our own training program for each day. We concentrated on the same program of weapons, scouting, and patrolling that had been developed previously. I wanted to bring in the new replacements and blend them into the unit, and I felt that these simple programs did just that. One day, we took the company down into the valley bottom to the Pool Table battle site at the crossing of the Volturno River. The main purpose of the trip was to show the new men where each platoon had fought and to have the veterans tell them what they did in battle. It was probably the most effective training day this company would ever have in Italy.

Staff Sgt. Ted Dahle, the mess sergeant, was a focal point of the company. His kitchen crew played an important and necessary role in developing the "soul" of the company—its morale. Sgt. Dahle was quiet in manner and twinkled with humor; he put together the most, and the best, meals. The sergeant ranged about to find extra items to add to the menus. His assistant, Sgt. Naughton from Williamsburg, Iowa, was our entertainer, musician, and joke-teller; he was someone we could all depend on. Also in the kitchen force was Cpl. Ken Lien, whose personal strengths were dependability and calmness. He had a handsome smile. Cpl. Looney was the opposite, in personality, of Sgt. Naughton. His role in life was to tell anyone who would listen his ideas on the futility of war. He said that war was like a huge meat chopper or grinder, with generals running the crank and handle and NCOs pushing the men into the top. Like the rest of us, however, he was contributing to the total effort to keep moving north until Hitler was destroyed. The men knew this was the only way to go before we could get back home.

Some of the veterans who had never been to a rest center in the "way back" rear got a chance to go there during this time. My name popped up on some kind of list, over which I had no control, so I spent a few days in Sorrento with its music, girls, and oranges you could pluck from the trees. I had a portrait of myself—a chalk pastel—done by an accomplished Italian artist.[1]

By the end of the last day of December, we were ready to head north again.

Around 5 January 1944, Company C entered into the line at night, along with the rest of the 133rd Infantry Regiment and a paratrooper force. We spent the initial days as reserve for the force. We were now in alpine country, above the tree line, in freezing weather. Snow and rocks served as the base for our footing. Generally, no trails existed, so walking was slow going. It was so cold that one night I slept on a rock boulder to keep out of the snow and put the boots I was wearing in a running mountain stream to keep my feet from freezing.

After moving probably some twenty zigzagging miles in this high mountain country, we finally engaged the enemy. My recollection of the tactical situation is scanty since we were following in reserve with no particular mission to accomplish except to move on farther to the north.

The enemy held the tallest and last mountains in the range. When our forces took these mountains, the enemy would be forced to fall back through the Cassino Valley for his next defensive line in the mountains to the north.

These final tall mountains were Hills 1109 and 1270. Based on my memory, the 133rd Infantry Regiment attacked these last two strongholds, with the 3rd battalion on the left and the

[1] *The pastel is reproduced on the back cover of the dust jacket.*

Sketch 4

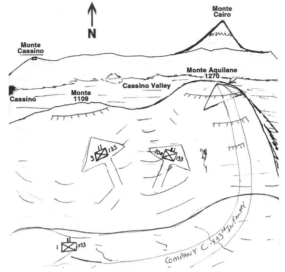

MONTE ACQUILINE, WINTER BATTLE, JANUARY 1944

100th Battalion to the right. To look at Hills 1109 and 1270 was like looking at half a bowl from inside the bowl. Hill 1270 is 1,270 meters—or about 4,000 feet—high.

I can only pick up the story at the point when Lt. Col. Eugene L. Moseley, the 1st Battalion commander, called his company commanders together late in the afternoon—it was almost at dark—to issue combat orders for the next day, 12 January 1944.

Col. Moseley quickly issued his order: "The 1st Battalion will attack from its regimental reserve position to seize the right of the regimental sector, the highest point, Hill 1270. The other two battalions will continue to attack in their zones. The 1st Battalion will attack, with Company C in the assault and the other two rifle companies in reserve. Company D[2] will be in support."

I requested permission from Col. Moseley to break away from this session in order to rush, in the limited daylight, to reconnoiter and see what had to be accomplished. It was always very important to me to learn all that I could determine about

[2] *A weapons company.*

the enemy and the terrain before issuing attack orders.

With about thirty minutes of daylight remaining and half a mile across the front to the right flank of the 100th Battalion, I moved quickly into our new attack area and into position to see three enemy defensive areas up the mountain that we had to attack. The first area was an enemy bunker about 200 yards away, the second area contained three enemy bunkers, and the third had five enemy bunkers. The bunkers looked solid, not hastily built. The steep slopes to these bunkers angled up about thirty degrees. Stone and snow would provide us with no real camouflage or cover if we made a frontal assault.

Frontal assaults were always the last option for me in designing an attack. First, I looked for flanks. The 100th Battalion occupied the left flank, so that was out. Moving to the right to see if that could be the flank route, I was disappointed to see that the enemy had skillfully placed his left flank on a steep escarpment that could not be climbed by our troops. Adding to my problem, this newly discovered escarpment gave me such a narrow area to attack that I could maneuver only one platoon forward in the assault echelon; therefore, my firepower in the assault would be very limited.

As darkness fell, I turned to the rear, behind the new assault line, and climbed down a slope. I found myself approaching a smaller hill about 300 yards from the first enemy bunker; I had found the tactical solution!

I rejoined the company at about 7:00 p.m. My orders to the platoon leader were as follows: "The regiment has attacked with two battalions and has not gained the regimental objectives of taking Hills 1109 and 1270. The 1st Battalion is now committed to the attack to seize 1270 and will attack to the regimental right side, right of the 100th Battalion. The 1st Battalion will attack with only company C in the assault. We will attack with 1st Lt. S. C. Tyrrell's rifle platoon in the assault, with the other two rifle platoons and weapons platoon in support by fire. Attack will be at 7:00 a.m." (See Sketch 5 of the scheme of maneuver.)

Sketch 5

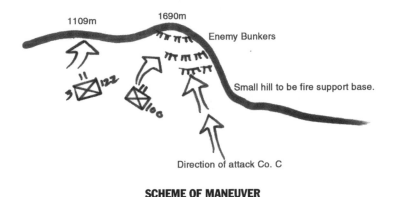

SCHEME OF MANEUVER

During the night, I moved the company to the small hill to be used as a fire support base. We allocated fires on every enemy position by ordering each platoon to fire on specified enemy bunkers. I told them to aim for the bunker openings. We moved Lt. Tyrrell's platoon forward to the area between the small hill and the enemy's first bunker. I would have battalion heavy weapons fire, all heavy machine guns, on the second and third bunker line, along with my own 60-mm mortars and machine guns. No artillery was to be used because the artillery units were unable to move in this alpine land of no trails. All was in order for the 7:00 a.m. attack.

As planned, the next morning—at 7:00 a.m. –I ordered all weapons to begin firing. All 100 or so riflemen and all other weapons began a heavy fire when Lt. Tyrrell, a new replacement officer, was given the signal to attack. The lieutenant jumped up and said, "Charge!" Then he started singing out loud, "Pistol-Packing Mama," a new stateside song we had never heard. I told him to halt and get his men back in the starting positions. We halted all other company and battalion firing and delayed the attack to 7:15 a.m.

Quickly I told Lt. Tyrrell two things: 1) He was going to get all of his men—some thirty plus—killed with his unorthodox "Chinese" attack drill, and 2) we never told platoon leaders how to attack but we were going to do so now. He would attack with one squad—ten to twelve men. His other two squads would fire in support to cover his assault by one squad.

From my viewpoint, this was a regimental attack; its three battalions had been committed. My battalion was attacking with one rifle company of its three; C Company was attacking with one rifle platoon of its three; the rifle platoon in assault was attacking with one squad of its three. In summary, one squad was to do the entire regimental job. Would it work? You bet it would work!

With every man in Company C firing his weapon in support, Lt. Tyrrell and the squad took the first enemy bunker. One of our men was killed by enemy fire. The assault squad fired as it moved into the enemy position, killing three of the enemy.

I rushed the lieutenant's two remaining squads to the newly seized position. I then told Lt. Tyrrell to take one of those two squads and attack the three bunkers on the next line. We now concentrated all fires on two remaining enemy lines. The next three enemy bunkers were taken in minutes with no friendly losses and about a dozen enemy killed or captured. We found that the Germans had reinforced their bunkers with steel beams and rock.

Again, I rushed the two squads that were held back in support firing positions forward to the newest seized positions and told Lt. Tyrrell to take the squad that had not been in any assault wave to attack the last line of the five enemy bunkers. I massed all company and battalion heavy weapons on the last line. The next and final enemy line was assaulted, all positions were taken, and, again, there were no friendly losses. Total enemy killed or captured was approximately fifty men. The entire attack took less than thirty minutes and was accomplished with our own infantry weapons.

Lt. Col. Moseley, a fine West Point officer, congratulated me in person after the battle. He proclaimed that, most likely, no other rifle company in World War II had ever attacked such a strong enemy position with such precision, using minimum assault forces and maximum firepower that was organic to the rifle company.

We had attained our near perfect rifle company warfare in the mountains. It was not perfect since we sustained the loss of one very good man.

Company C came off Hill 1270 victorious. The battalion became the advance guard and moved toward and down into the Cassino Valley, chasing the retreating enemy. We moved on a single mountain trail in a west/northwest direction. By noon, we had moved five to seven miles and had come to the first village in the immediate foothills of the south side of the Cassino Valley. Our company led the battalion.

We expected the Italians in the village to welcome us with joy, and we were right. They were joyous but very excitable and concerned about us. The best we could understand was their warning, *"Tedeski no comput"* (the Germans did not leave). We became more careful as we turned to a northerly route. The company was still in a single-file column as we followed a trail.

I halted the company to talk with the leading platoon leader. I warned him to proceed with caution since we did not know where the enemy was located. Although it seemed odd to me, since we were heading downhill and the ground advantage was ours, I directed a scouting force to go to the next natural feature or bound, whichever the platoon leader directed. We would then move the remainder of the company forward as each bound was secured.

Watching the first scouting force movement, I was disappointed with the way in which it was conducted. With only two men, the scouting force was too small, and the platoon leader, on his own, rushed his platoon forward too soon. In general, the scouting force totally disregarded my directions and the prudence with which those directions were to be carried out.

I halted the company a second time to correct this platoon. The company was now in the lower hills, which had olive tree groves in all directions. These groves hindered, even more, our observation abilities. I cautioned the company again; the platoon had to move carefully. I watched in horror as the platoon I had just cautioned moved forward with no scouting force. The lead platoon went right into an enemy trap—a rear slope defense that could not be seen unless it had been scouted in detail. We had never encountered such a defense in our past campaigns, but it was skillfully planned and executed by the German army on this day. The enemy massed his firepower on his rear slope rather than the conventional way of firing weapons on forces attacking their forward slope.

The following sketch depicts this battlefield situation:

Sketch 6

Co. C attack route

Profile of the rear slope

Stone terrace walls (10'-12')

OLIVE ORCHARD BATTLEFIELD

The olive orchards were terraced as shown in Sketch 6. The aged terraced walls were often ten to sixteen feet high and some 100 yards apart. Our front troops could only see over one terrace step at a time. The enemy had machine guns behind certain walls. As we advanced and our men got down a wall, the enemy would open fire, keeping the men from advancing further as well as keeping other men from assisting them. There was no way to move back and no way to escape from this fire since the wall was too high to climb quickly. Additionally, heavy enemy artillery fire from the Cassino Valley wreaked havoc as tree bursts spread shrapnel in an effective way upon all of us.[3]

The enemy artillery fires were brutal. I asked for help from the battalion for counter-artillery fire. Help came on my right flank when a sister company came up on line to relieve the pressure, but friendly artillery was not in position behind us since the mountain terrain was too rugged for it to be employed.

We lost Cpl. (probably then Sgt.) Ranney in this battle. Conscientious and thorough, he was the best overall squad leader of the company. He looked like a young minister, wore glasses, and was most thoughtful of his men. His death was a big loss to all of us. We lost Sgt. Barker here, too, but he was evacuated successfully. Fearless and brave, Sgt. Barker was the best combat squad leader of the company. He was from Minnesota. In addition to these men, we suffered other casualties as we "hunkered in" until dark. Due to the heavy and continuous artillery fire upon us, we were never able to maneuver our men.

The right flank was secured with another company up on line. Our left flank was exposed as a deep ravine led uphill to our flank, and a large stone Italian farmhouse stood there to be taken easily by the Germans. Flanking fire from the house would be fatal to us all.

First Sgt. Patrick told me he had five new replacements, two of whom were regular army sergeants, and he wanted to know what to do with them. "Send the senior sergeant to me," I replied. I gave this new sergeant an order to take these new men down to the left flank farmhouse and hold it until dark.

Continuing my tour of the company, I returned to see that the sergeant had not moved his small force as he had been directed. I told him that I knew he was a regular army sergeant and that it was fully expected of him to carry out orders. He said,

---

[3] *We visited this battlefield in 1984. The scars from enemy artillery fire in these aged olive trees verified the intensity of it all. It was easy to see how the Germans conducted this unusual defense so effectively. Some walls had a trail next to them that allowed the Germans to move their forces back and forth along the wall area from where they were firing, then back to another wall to set up additional defensive lines.*

"Lieutenant, I have never disobeyed an order, but I am scared to death!" Realizing that he was fully frightened, I helped him get his men together to go with me to the farmhouse. I stayed awhile to reassure them. These two sergeants turned out to be top leaders in the future.

By nightfall, on this short winter day, the enemy withdrew and the battle was over.

To go from a real victory to this encounter in less than twelve hours was leveling. It was not good that it turned out this way. The enemy had taught us a lesson; a rear slope defense is formidable because you cannot see it beforehand and are sucked into its trap. This one was skillfully conducted by our opponents in the German army.

Was the company's venture into the Cassino Valley a prelude of things to come? Was this to be a valley of pure hell?[4]

---

[4] *We revisited this valley in 1984. Even then, because of my memories of what had happened there, the valley did not appear peaceful.*

The Battle at Cassino
Italy, 1944

The floor of the Cassino Valley is wide and mostly open. The German "Gustav Line" was based on the wall of mountains surrounding the valley. The line started at its western end with the city of Cassino and the Monte Cassino Abbey and stretched eastward to the distant base of the snow-capped Mount Cairo.

When we arrived in the area, the valley floor was flooded, making it possible only for infantry to penetrate, and even that

Sketch 7

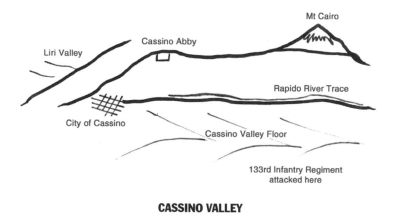

CASSINO VALLEY

was done with difficulty. Useless in the flooded area, our tanks could not join us in the planned attack.

The first stab at the enemy for Company C was to be a feint company frontal attack of the city of Cassino, located at the base of the mountain below the abbey. Engineers and engineer boats joined us in our night approach. The boats were heavy and cumbersome, making them difficult to move by hand carriers and thereby slowing us down. The rest of the company was ready to move swiftly, but we had to stop frequently to allow the boats to catch up. From my point of view, this created a nightmare attack situation. The feint attack occurred on 21 or 22 January 1944.

The next morning, as we successfully moved this force back without attracting enemy artillery fire, I had an experience that enhanced my morale. In the field, a regimental runner representing the regimental commander, Col. Ray Fountain, approached me and presented me with a set of captain bars, along with the colonel's congratulations. I was twenty-two years old on that promotion day.

Events happened quickly after that. The next day, Allied forces landed at Anzio to establish a beachhead behind the Germans at Cassino. Over the next two days, our regiment moved to the east to be in position to make a frontal attack on the Cassino Mountain wall on 24 January 1944.

Monte Cassino Abbey

We sent our patrols north to the Rapido River. One of the patrol leaders, Sgt. Ascona, provided us with the most useful information. He had found the Rapido River almost bone dry because the Germans had diverted its waters laterally into the valley. Sgt. Ascona had traversed the banks of the river trying to find any area between the river and the mountain base that was not mined, but he found all areas to be heavily mined with anti-personnel mines.

Our attack forward started at night, near midnight. Our own artillery was brilliant as it covered the entire huge dark wall of mountains to our front with continuous bursting fire. It was great to see the enemy-held mountain covered with fire, but the Germans had dug into rock and had reinforced their positions overhead with steel and rock.

Did our artillery fire do any good? It did not stop the enemy from firing his defensive artillery barrages as we approached. One of the first reports I received was that a company soldier, a name I have, unfortunately, long since forgotten, had been killed when he ducked into a haystack, which received a direct hit.

As we approached the Rapido River, it became more difficult to move. The enemy had diverted water from the river into deep narrow ditches, which ran in all directions. The water was waist-deep and ran swiftly, and we all became soaked, at least to the waist. I was completely wet after stepping in a hole that I couldn't see in a dark ditch. We were all miserably wet and cold when we arrived at the Rapido River just before daybreak.

The river, a small stream with banks eight to ten feet high, ran its course some 400 yards from the base of Cassino Mountain, which had a large, menacing shoulder that protruded south of the main mass. This shoulder promised to be a key defensive area for the Germans since it protected a front wider than the shoulder itself. A minefield with signs saying "*Minen*" lay all along our front. The land was flat, and all the trees had been cut down.

We searched for openings through the minefield. The most promising area was on the extreme left flank where an incom-

Col. Wilkinson in 1984 at minefield site

ing mountain stream flowed from a section designated on a map as the "Italian Barracks" area. I ventured forward at the left edge of a clearing where the enemy had cut down sapling trees in mass and had placed mines and trip wires throughout their branches. I saw a mine trip-wire across my approach route and froze. Then I heard an incoming enemy artillery shell. My ears had become keen in judging the closeness of artillery shells, and this one was going to be close! I dived forward, parallel to the ground, hurling myself over the trip-wire to take cover in a large shell-hole, just beyond the wire. But my heavy, soaked boots and clothes caused me to drag the wire, and the mine exploded. Since it was the type that would lift up in the air a few feet before detonating, shrapnel pierced my back. If I had been standing, the explosion would have been fatal.[1] My wound felt superficial; I was wet and miserable, but still mobile, so I never examined it.

We could not find any area that was not mined, and I would not order these men to go through a minefield without assistance. For the first and only time in my career, I decided that I

[1] *In 1984, Corny and I retraced this same route from the river. When we were within fifty feet of this spot and were looking ahead, I announced, "If we could find ahead the remains of the large shell hole that I dived for, surely this would be the spot!" Amazingly, we found the depression of that old shell hole! It marked the spot where I had been wounded.*

would go to the rear and talk to my next commander about the situation that faced us all.

I went back to the battalion headquarters to ask Lt. Col. Moseley for engineering assistance to help us get through the minefield. He was agreeable and immediately called Col. Marshall at regimental headquarters. Col. Marshall was not helpful, but at Lt. Col. Moseley's request, he did give him permission to speak to Gen. Ryder, the division commander. Since I was standing beside Col. Moseley as he began to talk on the phone, I suggested that since Gen. Ryder "owned" the tanks, Col. Moseley should ask for tanks to fire directly on the enemy machine guns that I had spotted to my front. I thought that even though the tanks could not reach the river, they could be effective from a thousand yards back. Col. Moseley requested from Gen. Ryder both engineer and tank support. The general said he could provide the engineers but not tanks in our support.

After I returned to the company, which was on line at the river, I had the men improve the firing positions that were located into the forward riverbank and then had them to fire on the three enemy positions. We had casualties from enemy artillery fire, which was almost continuous.

Sketch 8

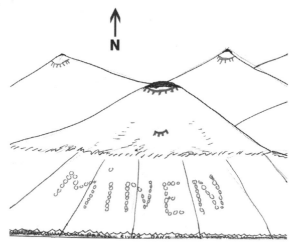

THE MINEFIELD

At midmorning the next day, a lanky engineer lieutenant reported to me. His mission was to clear the minefield. I had wanted, and expected, a small crew to do the job since we needed at least two clear lanes to go forward, but with only one person, I had to settle for one cleared path. The day was cloudy, foggy, and drizzly, which proved to be beneficial to us. Our job was to advance about 200 yards through the minefield and straight into the face of three machine guns, 300 yards away. The enemy could fire down on us from heights of 300 to 500 feet. Clearing a path for us would be a tedious, time-consuming job since the engineer only had a hunting knife with which to probe for mines and engineering tape to mark the cleared path. At any time we could expect enemy fire, at least from the machine guns.

One platoon of riflemen covered our advance with fire from their weapons. Two platoons moved forward in single file with large intervals between men. I stationed myself behind the engineer, at the head of the company file. Corny was behind me, followed by the platoons. My plan was to reach the base of the mountain by dark and to make a night attack on the gun positions.

The engineer officer was very patient and carefully traced each wire he found to a mine. I really do not know what he did with the mines he found since I was hugging the ground. Our men marked the sides of the cleared path with white cotton tapes.

When would the enemy machine guns begin firing? We provided them with an ideal target. The men behind me, however, presented minimum targets. I could not see them from my various positions because of the maze of branches that were located everywhere about us and because we all crawled in prone positions, slithering through the mud.

By 3:00 p.m., the engineer officer had finished his job and was thanked and dismissed. Our next obstacle lay ahead. Before us we saw a double-aproned barbed-wire fence at the base of the mountain, about twenty yards away, blocking our approach. The first enemy machine gun was about forty-five degrees upward and over to the right about 100 yards away. My plan was for us to take that first gun so that the two following platoons could have a chance to come forward. Corny shot at the enemy gun to cover me as I dashed forward to the barbed wire, which had been damaged by our artillary fire, and leaped over it. In midair, I spotted a six-to-eight-inch rusty iron pipe stretched on the ground just beyond the wire. The pipe exploded with a roar, blowing me nearly back to the position from where I had started. Heavy enemy machine gun and mortar fire rained down when the iron pipe was blown. Corny and I both moved into adjoining deep shell holes, which were filled with mud and water, and fired on the machine gun. Mortar shell pounded into the earth all around us. As I lay prone on the ground, with my body flat under mud and water, one shell landed about a foot from my head. I waited for my head to be blown off my body! But the shell didn't explode! I looked up and saw the mud settling over it. I was saved! Thank the Lord!

At nightfall we wandered back through the tape-lined path. We didn't find any bodies or wounded in the path, but we had taken some casualties.

Back with Lt. Col. Moseley that night, I received another attack order for the next day. Col. Moseley announced that he would lead the attack, and I assured him that Company C would be right with him. He also told me that he had asked to be relieved after the battle was over. I was shocked because I believe that a commander of troops should never ask ahead of time to be relieved after a battle has ended. The troops cannot have confidence in a mission with such a cloud hanging over the orders.

The next day, I took Col. Moseley to the spot at the riverbank where our single, cleared path began through the minefield. Company C had eight riflemen, who were my force. All of these men had bloody left hands as a result of hitting the M-1 bolt handle so many times to get their mud-clogged rifles to fire.[2] The colonel had no fire plan, and his maneuver plan

---

[2] *Normally, they would have fired semi-automatically.*

was to go straightforward to the enemy's positions through the cleared path.

True to his word, Moseley led this very futile and fatal attack. He stepped out of the river and up to the bank top, then toppled back right in front of me. He had been shot through the forehead and was instantly killed. We all fired our weapons from the banks in anger and futility, a final salute to a very brave soldier. His death was tragic.

The final act of battle for the 1st Battalion occurred in that dreadful place by the enemy minefield.

We moved to the left to line up with other soldiers so our next attack would be against the Italian army barracks area at the mountain base.

Corny and I went on a reconnaissance before this attack and found ourselves in a battered stone farmhouse in an open field. We went upstairs to find a better observation point of the enemy positions, and shortly thereafter an enemy artillery observer, positioned somewhere in the distant mountains, decided to blast us with artillery fire. Shells hit the roof and blew tiles off as we hastily retreated to the ground floor for more protection. In a subsequent artillery volley, fragments coming through an open window struck Corny on the arm. We bandaged his wound, and even though he didn't want to go, I told him to take off to the rear for help at the medical-aid station. I watched him race across the field with enemy shells trying to hit him. Fortunately, he made a safe escape.

Minutes later, I looked to the rear to see enemy shells hitting the field. Inside the barrage was Corny running back to join me. When he got to the farmhouse, he said in a panting voice, "Captain, I wanted to tell you goodbye; I forgot to do that before."

"Thanks, Corny," I said, "but you get the hell out of here and get your arm fixed." Corny recovered from the arm wound and returned to action with his company.

Rejoining the company that night, I found that the back wound I had sustained the previous day had become infected. I was unable to raise myself from the ground where I slept. Kind and thoughtful, my soldiers made a blanket stretcher and carried me in it the next day. If they stumbled and fell, they would make any body movement necessary to keep my body from striking the rocky ground.

Medics at a nearby tented evacuation hospital operated on the wound to clean it, using sulfur powder to fight the infection. I don't remember much about my time in the hospital, but I do remember telling the nurse that I was cold and tired. She placed my cot next to a cherry-red pot-bellied stove. I got warm and slept for days, it seemed. The metal shrapnel remained in my body. For the next month, I convalesced at a general hospital in Naples.

Upon being dismissed, my orders were to report to a nearby replacement depot. The people there told me to go draw combat equipment and to take a combat course. That was one course that this soldier did not need! My next move was to walk out the gate and to find a 34th Division truck to take me back to the front.

The front was still the Cassino battle area. Company C would be pulled from the line at Cassino city in two days, so we made plans with the kitchen and supply forces to be prepared to greet and feed the troops and to provide them with new uniforms, other items of clothing, and various goods.

Our troops moved in silently at night. The next morning we had a joyous reunion—and a huge breakfast of all the pancakes we could eat. Our biggest man, Sgt. Holub, told me that he still did not have enough to eat, so I got Staff Sgt. Dahle to make a pancake as large as the griddle, at least four feet by four feet, which was folded over and over again and smothered with butter and syrup. The whole company watched and cheered as Sgt. Holub ate it all and finally proclaimed that he was full! Even after the ordeal of combat, the men in this company had a basic spirit of comradeship and devotion to each other that was outstanding. It was also our salvation.

After the sojourn in the city of Cassino, we all went back about thirty or forty miles to the same Piedmont d'Alife area where we had been in December. The company returned to Samuel Lumbar's olive orchard. We remained there long enough for men to go to rest and recreational areas. Then we prepared to move to the Anzio beachhead.

Postscript

I would like to take time, now, to recognize two outstanding soldiers of Company C.

Frank G. "Snuffy" Graham

One great "morale builder" soldier was the company's jeep driver, Frank G. "Snuffy" Graham from Lakeland, Minnesota. Snuffy had a young, "big-eyed," laughing face with a happy, mouth-filled drawl developed in southern Minnesota.

Snuffy's combat role was to bring up the supplies each night to our newest seized positions. He always found us and often risked his life doing so, driving many nights back and forth with no lights and no one to clear enemy mines in the new roads and trails that he took. Frequently, he rushed across open spaces where enemy artillery tried to "bump" him off. He was fearless and dependable.

Nightly, Snuffy rolled in on the top or bottom of the newly seized mountain with the motor roaring, his steel helmet down almost to his shoulders (he alone in the unit wore no helmet liner), a grin on his face, and his eyes rolling. He told so many tall tales about his trip that even seasoned old soldiers who had had a bad day fighting the enemy felt that Snuffy had had a worse day.

Snuffy delivered our mail, and that brought cheers from the men. Additionally, he brought us rations, water, and gasoline, and he was a hero when, starting in 1944, we received hunks of roast beef and large laundry bags filled with fresh quartermaster bread—that was good bread! He also delivered ammunition and parts for weapons. But mainly he brought himself, a real soldier who did not let his fellow man down.

Snuffy's jeep had more Purple Hearts than did an entire squad of soldiers. When the jeep wore out, Snuffy took a trip into the nearest British army sector. The British had new U. S.

jeeps, and he traded up; one jeep of ours for one of theirs. He would bring back the new jeep, which bore the hood of the old jeep since the old one had the necessary number and lettering that identified it as ours. Those trades took some doing!

Eldon D. Johnson

I now want to pay tribute to a very special soldier, who was with the company from 1941 to 1945. He was one of the few men in the combat areas of the company from start to finish— from Tunisia to the Swiss border. His was the communications sergeant, Eldon D. Johnson from Ceder Rapids, Iowa.

Eldon had a youthful face that made him look much younger than his real age in the mid-twenties. His had a very serious demeanor that contrasted with an easy smile. He had the technical responsibility for all communications within the company and kept the maps and records of where we went and what time we went to various places. He also kept the radio's runners and telephone lines in action. He and his men performed impeccably in this very important and necessary task.

I was fortunate to return to Italy in 1984 with Eldon Johnson, Leighton McKeithan, and Everett "Corny" Cornelius. Eldon had our trip so organized that every route taken in 1943, 1944, and 1945 was logged and plotted on wartime maps. We followed those maps completely and practically, to and through all of the battlefields of the past.

Since World War II and until his death around the turn of the century, Eldon was active in communicating with Company C veterans and was responsible for our large attendance at many reunions. He was also active in 34th Division affairs, projects, and history. He sponsored, along with Jerry Snoble and Kenny Lien, annual company reunions every fall in Iowa and wrote extensively about C Company.

Eldon contributed much to keep the spirit of Company C intact and alive. We are all thankful to him for his untiring work and dedication.

8

The Defense of the Anzio Beachhead
Italy, 1944

Allied forces had landed at Anzio during the initial stages of the Cassino battle. The grand design had been to go around and behind the German line with this landing, thus forcing the Germans to abandon their defensive Gustav Line, which was anchored at Cassino.

The grand design had failed for two main reasons. The first reason was that the Army Corps commander, Gen. Lucas, had misgivings about his beachhead mission and felt that he and this mission were doomed from the beginning. The Army commander, Gen. Clark, issued the operations order, which directed Gen. Lucas to land at Anzio and to "advance on the Alban Hills," which led to Rome and blocked the enemy supply lines to the Cassino front. The cautious use of the word "on" instead of "to" reinforced Gen. Lucas's lack of aggressiveness. In effect, the landing was unopposed.

The second reason for failure was that the movement "on" the Alban Hills was not a bold thrust. The Germans quickly saw the Allied mistake and rushed forces to seize all of the high ground—Alban Hills—and to counterattack. For a month, the battle was bitter, and the Allies[1] bravely held a beachhead. This battle lasted from late January into February and early March.

The 34th Infantry Division was moved onto the beachhead in the last half of March 1944. The 133rd Infantry Regiment was the last regiment of the division to move by ship from Naples to Anzio.

Our movement was uneventful, and initially our regiment was the division reserve. The division had a defensive area on the right extreme corner of the beachhead line.

After a three- to four-day stay in the reserve, the 133rd Regiment relieved the division's 168th Infantry Regiment on the front line.

Company C relieved a sister company of the 168th Infantry in the smoothest, most professional relief one could hope to accomplish. These two seasoned units of company size accomplished the relief with speed, precision, and attention to detail that I have never seen surpassed. Perhaps one thing was paramount: the 168th Rifle Company was not rushing to get relieved, as units are often prone to do, and they were proud of their fortifications. Their design of, and improvement to, the fortifications had made them a superb defensive line.

Our defensive line was on the elevated banks of the Mussolini Canal. The banks of the canal stood a good twenty to thirty feet above the surrounding fields, and the land was flat to the eastern side of the mountains that were held by the enemy. The two banks of the canal plus the canal basin itself were 300 to 400 feet across, and the defensive front was 3,000 yards wide. This meant that every two men had to cover about fifty yards. Attached to us was a 60-mm mortar platoon[2] to help us cover such an extended front. We had twelve light machine guns in addition to the two weapons regularly assigned to us. Both Germans and Americans had placed mine fields across our front. An additional characteristic of this defensive line was

[1] *American and British forces.*

[2] *American Neisi (Japanese-Americans from Hawaii) troops.*

our location next to the right angle turn to the main beach-head line. We were defending on a line that generally ran east and west. Our sister rifle company on our left defended on a line that ran north and south. Both companies received enemy artillery fire from their fronts, flanks, and rear. Since the enemy held the high ground, they had positions from which they could observe our flanks and rear during daylight hours.

Sketch 9

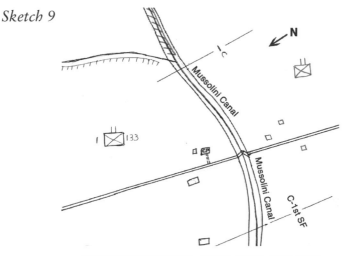

COMPANY C DEFENSE - ANZIO, APRIL-MAY 1944

Our command post was a farmhouse 400 feet behind the Mussolini Canal. Daylight movement around the house was impossible without attracting enemy artillery fire. Consequently, all of our movements were made at night.

Our previous defenders—the 168th Infantry Regiment—and the opposing Germans had reached an agreement on an outpost line. Each held farmhouses so close to each other that they could almost verbally communicate with each other. Both forces occupied certain outposts only at night.

My own basic military philosophy was to attack. I was not inclined to be defensive-minded, so the sooner we got out of this situation, the better I thought it would be. My goal was not to be in front of the enemy but to be on his flanks, or, best of all, to be at his rear. At his rear, I could use our artillery and maneuver to surprise him. But being at the enemy's front where he could use his artillery on us was not a comforting feeling.

All in all, at this location, the war was quiet in many ways. We could not aggressively patrol or probe the enemy because no one knew where the minefields were located. Possibly we were too strong for the enemy to risk attacking us. From the German viewpoint, then, we were in a quiet sector: we were on the opposite side of the beachhead from Rome, and the German priority was to keep us from advancing to Rome.

Our troops and the German troops patrolled at night. Occasionally, I received information about the German patrols in our rear. One night, I learned that one of our patrols had not returned on schedule. Early the next morning, PFC Leighton "Mac" McKeithan, a member of one of the front-line platoons, presented himself to me and requested permission to go alone on a daylight patrol "to find my sergeant, if he can be found." The target of his search would be Sgt. Rodriquez, a Spanish-American professional sergeant who was missing with his small patrol.

I explained to Mac the seriousness of his proposed mission, but he said that he wanted to go and mentioned that he could carry a handmade Red Cross flag with him. I agreed and made plans to cover him with rifle fire if he became endangered. Mac was a very brave soldier to attempt this mission, and he was influenced by his own very deep respect and admiration for Sgt. Rodriquez, a real soldier who was a masterful platoon sergeant.

Pvt. McKeithan followed the same route into "no-man's-land" that the patrol had taken, but he had to turn back when the Germans told him not to advance any further. We were all saddened that we could not learn the fate of Sgt. Rodriquez.[3]

---

[3] *In 1984, McKeithan, Corny, Eldon Johnson, and I visited Anzio and the beautiful American cemetery there. We left dried flowers, which we had picked earlier at Anzio and other Company C battlefields, on the graves of the company men resting there in peace. There we found Sgt. Rodriquez's grave, which we dutifully covered with flowers, and we all said a prayer for him. We never learned the circumstances of his death.*

While we were on the front lines, we created our own entertainment. The Germans helped by dropping propaganda leaflets over us each morning for about a week. The subject of these leaflets, which were printed on small, light-colored tissue and looked like coupon-shaped tickets, was Joan, the beautiful, blonde girl back home waiting for her beloved soldier to return. Each day the leaflets got "hotter." Joan went to work as a secretary, and her boss got fresher each day, stripping off more and more of her clothes. The day she was down to "baring it all" was fully expected by all of us, but the leaflets blew into no-man's-land! That didn't stop the men of this company though! All of them left their positions and charged forward to retrieve the leaflets. For a brief time, we had lost control of an entire company of men. Of course, they returned immediately, clutching the prized leaflets. As a result of their forage into no-man's-land, though, we knew where there were no mines!

Near the farmhouse was a grain shed filled about waist deep with shelled yellow corn. One of our cooks, "Tennessee" Lawson, was an expert on making corn whiskey. I told Staff Sgt. Dahle to make a limited amount of booze, in secret, back at the kitchen area. The limit would be a jar each day for each platoon and headquarters, a total of five jars, as well as an additional jar for the rear force at the kitchen area. I told him that if he made more than that, I would have his hide. The five jars of "white lightening" arrived with the rations and water each night. When I queried the platoons on how it worked out, I was told it was received with pleasure by the soldiers more than twenty years old, but most of the ones under twenty didn't want to imbibe. The booze never led to any disciplinary problems.

The men made razor blade radios with copper wire, a razor blade, a block of wood, and a set of headphones. They tuned in "Axis Sally," a German radio station designed to lower American morale. It built ours up!

My major battle was with my next superior headquarters, the battalion. A new commander was in charge, a fresh lieutenant colonel straight from the Infantry School at Fort Benning, Georgia. He was a self-proclaimed expert on infantry weaponry. I can't remember his name, but it seems to me that it rhymed with "Nixon." Maybe it was Hixon or maybe Hix.

Nonetheless, each night for days on end, I received a call to report to this commander. I had to trek toward the back through random enemy artillery fire and zigzag at least two miles to reach his headquarters. Each night, he challenged my map overlay location of one of my dozen-plus machine guns. He wanted me to move a gun a night a few feet, in one direction or another, to get what he called the "maximum best position." My arguments that I had physically placed each gun in its best position did not mean a thing to him. We moved "dots" on map overlays that showed new gun positions, but we never moved a weapon. Each was located in the best-camouflaged and protected position to cover the area with the best field of fire, to have the best chance to be re-supplied under fire, and to provide the best chance for a wounded machine gunner to get to safety.

I invited the colonel to visit our company and to see for himself where our machine guns were placed. Since he had never been to my area on the front, I thought that perhaps he could learn from us or share with us his knowledge of weaponry. My strategy worked. After issuing the invitation, I received no further requests to make nightly visits to his headquarters to discuss this matter.

After dusk many days later, the kitchen crew delivered the rations, including the whiskey, to our farmhouse. Our job was to divide it into the platoon packages based on a daily count of the number of men in each platoon. First Sgt. Patrick, Corny, Sgt. Eldon Johnson, myself, and any others we had been able to find were at this task when a person headed toward us down the lane to the farm area. We challenged him to "Halt!" but he kept coming. A quickly issued second order to halt also proved ineffective in stopping the approaching figure. Sgt. Patrick pulled his 45 pistol and asked, "Captain, can I shoot?"

I had to make a quick decision. The person was now nearing a hand-grenade-throwing position. Alerting everyone to lie low and be ready, I barked "Halt!" He stopped but failed my next challenge of giving me the counter to the password. Then I deduced that the stranger was actually the new colonel, and I walked out to him and said, "Colonel, we mean business here. We start shooting when people don't halt on our commands and don't know the passwords." He muttered, turned about, and left. The colonel never saw our machine gun positions!

The humor we developed during this time was rather twisted. We cheered the German "Anzio Express" 280-mm shells that whizzed overhead as we moved toward the port areas of the beachhead. We knew—and were joyful—that the shells had missed us by twenty miles. We delighted in setting up a TOT (time on target) of our own: a stone privy visited each morning at precisely the same time by a methodical German soldier. On my order, every big gun on the beachhead fired one round at this ridiculous target. When the dust settled, we had not directly hit the privy, and the German soldier calmly walked away. But he didn't return the next day!

Upstream from us in the Mussolini Canal, ten to twelve German soldiers would bathe in the canal and wash their clothes. My men wanted to shoot them, but I wouldn't allow them to do so. However, I did tell them that we would put the same number of men out at the same time to bathe and wash their clothes. At that rate, it took several days for all of my men to bathe.

The first day of May was a special day for the Japanese-American mortar platoon that we had attached to us, and they invited several of us to a noontime Hawaiian banquet. A room in that platoon's farmhouse was covered with woven blankets of green grass and wildflowers, leaving the floor, walls, and ceiling beautiful. The table, which was matted in the same fashion, held huge bowls of soups made from green wild plants seasoned with meat from "K" rations. We were greeted with Hawaiian music, leis, and other native gestures. It was a wonderful event for us.

Even as we celebrated with our friends, we were in the process of preparing for a big offensive to break out from the beachhead and to take the city of Rome from the south. In all of its history, Rome had never been taken from the south. At that time, we had to make the mental adjustment of moving from a defensive to an offensive mode of warfare. Fortunately, offense seemed to be the nature of these soldiers I commanded.

The Battle of the Wild-Flowered Soldiers
Italy, 1944

Early May 1944 brought with it blossoms of magnificent wildflowers that bloomed in carpets of tufted grass, which had not been grazed because of the war. This peaceful, pastoral scene was the site for the explosive attack of the American and British forces to break out of the Anzio beachhead during the period of 20-22 May 1944.

Company C was the last line company of the battalion to be relieved of its defense along the Mussolini Canal. The other two rifle companies of the battalion were defensively located on the axis of the attack and thus were engaged on 20 May to attack frontally and secure a line of departure for the 1st Special Forces. The mission of this force was to seize the main coastal Highway No. 7 and then take a parallel, elevated railroad track about 600 yards to the east.

The mission of the 1st Battalion was to follow in the support of the 1st Special Forces and to be prepared to attack, on orders, through that force. The 1st Special Forces enjoyed a reputation of having the combat power of a force larger than an infantry regiment.

On a beautiful sunny morning, Company C had moved forward of the old beachhead defensive line and was dispersed in an assembly area, which lay in a sunken ravine of the Cisterna Creek, among a few scattered trees, tall green grass, and flowers.

The battle raged in front of us, but the scattered trees on the flat terrain blocked our view, and we couldn't see what action the men of the assaulting 1st Special Forces were taking.

Soon after noon that day, I received orders to prepare to attack through the 1st Special Forces and seize Highway No. 7 and the railroad tracks. The 1st Special Forces had taken these objectives but had been forced back to an area unknown to me. Immediately, I went forward to see if we could contact the elements of the force in order to obtain information about the enemy's positions and strength. Meanwhile, the company was alerted to the new attack.

As I moved forward a distance of approximately 500 to 800 yards to a large drainage ditch area that ran diagonally across the front, I came upon a sad sight. The remnants of the 1st Special Forces were gathered there—several hundred men wounded or dying, with those few men who were able providing aid to the suffering. It was the worst and bloodiest wartime scene imaginable; I have never seen anything worse.

Moving about in the midst of this mass of men was a tall officer, whom I judged to be Brig. Gen. Frederick, the commanding general of the force. I reported to the general, told him who I was and what force I commanded, and relayed my mission to attack through his force to seize Highway No. 7 and the railroad tracks.

The general had tears in his eyes when he told me, "Look at my men." Everywhere up and down that ditch I saw wounded or dying soldiers. "I've lost most of my men, captain; you will never make it!"

I told him I was sorry about his men, then asked if he could he tell me the type of the enemy force and where it was located.

He said, "There are five tiger tanks behind the railroad tracks with the gun barrels lying across the rails." I asked him if the enemy was on Highway No. 7, and he said he felt that the Germans would have a minimum force there if any at all.

I saluted Gen. Frederick and departed with mixed feelings. First, I was impressed at seeing a general on the battlefield. I had never seen a general or, for that fact, even a full colonel on my battlefields in over one and a third years of combat. Second, I had deep respect for the 1st Special Forces and its attack abilities, but I also had deep respect for the attack abilities of Company C and had a plan on how to execute an attack that might have better results than the one that had just failed.

Joining the company in the assembly area, I received a shock of great proportions. During my absence, each man in Company C had made for himself a camouflage of flowers and grass. All of their helmets were covered with a heavy string net to reduce sun glare, but now, woven into these nets were natural grass and some flowers. They had also placed woven mats of the same green growth across their shoulders; these mats extended to the waists of some soldiers. The message these men were giving me was that they were ready to go!

Conferring with battalion headquarters, I requested an artillery rolling barrage, moving forward at a rate of 200 yards every five minutes. Our troops would move and lean against this barrage and sweep across Highway 7 and onto the railroad tracks. This was the plan I had envisioned when I talked to Gen. Frederick. My request for this fire support was honored, and the attack from a line of departure was set for 3:00 p.m. Company C would be the left attack company; Company B, the right attack company. This company was to anchor on the banks of the Mussolini Canal, which was perpendicular to the axis of attack.

At 3:00 p.m., Company C was at the line of departure, deployed with two rifle platoons[1] on line, dispersed and waiting for the rolling barrage to begin.

---

[1] *All squads.*

But the other attacking company was nowhere in sight. I called battalion headquarters to learn the location of that company and was told that the company would not be part of the attack.

I asked for my orders and received no answer other than I was to "hold."

I pressed again and again for orders and continued to get no response except that we were to hold.

Here was the situation. First, the company's men had mentally and physically prepared themselves for this attack. Second, to continue to hold up would drain the edge we had and ultimately destroy it. And third, to attain that edge again would be almost impossible under the circumstances of battle.

I called battalion headquarters and told them that Company C would attack alone if the rolling barrage was placed in front of us and a new and second barrage was placed where the other company should have been deployed in order to make the enemy think we had attacking troops on a wide front. This second barrage, on my right flank, would need to move in tandem with our movement. It would resemble the following sketch.

Sketch 10   ⟵ **N**

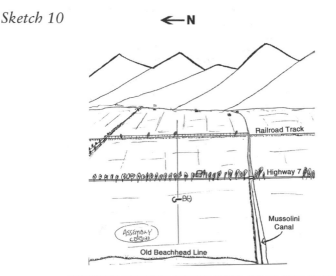

COMPANY C BREAKS OUT OF ANZIO, 20-22 MAY 1944

My request was approved, and shortly thereafter, the two barrages came down to our front and on our flank as requested. Our troops pressed as close as 50 to 75 yards from the front barrage. They moved swiftly forward as the barrage moved. I placed myself, with Corny and his radio, in the center, behind and between the two attacking platoons. The two continuous barrages of exploding shells concealed our troops from enemy view.

But a problem developed; just to the rear of Corny and me, one gun of the artillery unit that was firing in support kept shooting its rounds short, right behind us! These rounds were consistently short, moving forward as the barrage moved forward. Needless to say, they kept Corny and me on line! The men in front of us kept an eye on these short rounds, too, but I guess they figured that if we could take it, it had to be all right. Based on my experience, many infantry commanders would have halted the firing and demanded a check to correct the gun that was firing off target. I believe, though, that our attack was such a perfect display of overall precision that I could not halt and endure a lengthy delay to correct this error. After all, it was doing us no real harm and even spurred us on!

The attacking line continued to lean against the moving barrage and crossed Highway 7, followed by the 600-yard-wide open field between the highway and the railroad tracks. The box barrage was now perfect as it blasted the elevated tracks and their banks. Our soldiers moved into an assault position less than 100 yards from the tracks. I then called for the barrage to be moved 200 yards beyond the tracks so that we could make a final assault.

The firing stopped, and the assault was rapidly executed. Our men went over the elevated banks, across the tracks, and onto the far side of the tracks. I received reports of forty enemy soldiers captured and other Germans killed or wounded.

Then the wrong thing happened! The friendly barrage that I had requested 200 yards beyond the tracks came in, but in the wrong place. Friendly artillery fire rained down on the tracks where our men were mopping up the enemy. I called immediately to request that the firing be halted and then ordered the two platoons to move rapidly to the outside flanks and return to their original assault positions for a second assault. I told them to abandon their prisoners. The friendly barrage continued throughout this time.

Quickly, in not more than two to three minutes, the two platoons came back around each flank and assumed the assault position for the second time. Both lieutenants in charge signaled that they were ready to assault, and I gave them the go-ahead.

This time, the friendly artillery barrage landed 200 yards to the east and caught some enemy troops trying to flee. We seized two, maybe three, enemy tiger tanks and took a few prisoners. We had now seized and held our objective: the elevated railroad tracks.

Then another problem arose. One enemy tiger tank remained, and it was located to the right, about where the tracks crossed the Mussolini Canal. We knew it was there when it fired a tank round at Corny and me as we moved through an open field about 100 to 200 yards from the tracks. The round missed us, but it was close. The route we chose to gain cover led to a brick farmhouse located to our right rear, next to Highway No. 7 and several hundred yards away.

We ran as fast as we could with the enemy tank rounds barely missing us. I sprinted to the back of the building and captured a surprised German soldier who had flattened himself against the wall. Corny entered the front door of a garage area, which was directly exposed to the tank fire. I yelled at him to get back with me. It was a miracle that he made it back because he had to dash forward through the garage entrance, then turn the corner and come to my place at the back of the house.

The enemy tiger tank tried to kill us there. The brick building was too big and strong to destroy quickly, so he fired airbursts at us. The first burst was about 300 yards behind us. The next was 100 yards behind. Corny and I knew that if he came back another 100 yards, we would be killed. The enemy tanker tried to shorten the timing of the burst but wasn't able to do so.

We were saved!

I have always been amazed—and dismayed—that this very brave attack by Company C was never recognized. Most accounts note the 1st Special Forces as bravely making the same assault as we did but acknowledge that they were pushed back to the area west of Highway No. 7. Gen. Frederick had told me that we could not succeed, but we did—within four hours after I spoke with him.

By now, the battalion had a new commander. He indicated to me that he was embarrassed that the other rifle company did not attack according to the orders. He never congratulated Company C for its brilliant attack, and he implied that our efforts were never reported to the regiment. I told him that was his problem, not mine. Company C had done its job.

The company had sustained only very few casualties, and I say amen to that because we could have had more. I believe those few casualties came from our own artillery fire that fell in error on the railroad tracks.

10

The Battle of Lanuvio
Near Rome, Italy, 1944

The drive from the Anzio beachhead north to Rome was made in earnest the last day of May 1944. The obstacle for the 34th Division was the German "Caesar Line," anchored in the city of Lanuvio in the Alban Hills. The Germans had not hastily built this defensive line; rather, they methodically built it over a period of time, constructing numerous firing bunkers on the hilly terrain that were excellent for defense.

The 133rd Infantry hooked around and to the left of the city, approaching it from the east/northeast. The 3rd Battalion was committed initially, with the 1st Battalion following behind.

On the day the 3rd Battalion attacked, Maj. Dumont, the battalion commander, alerted me that he planned to attack soon from a rock quarry, moving uphill from the quarry toward the enemy defensive line. My initial response was to tell him that I would spend that day[1] on reconnaissance, moving forward from the 3rd Battalion area since I had very deep reservations about moving into a rock quarry to begin an attack. Surely, I thought, this would be a death-hole target for enemy artillery and mortar fire.

Corny and I began our reconnaissance by approaching the quarry itself. From a distance, it appeared to have a horseshoe shape with a narrow entrance on the west side. We approached with caution, covering each other as we advanced. Further to

---

[1] *Probably 31 May 1944.*

The quarry in 1984

our left, and at a distance of at least a mile, the 3rd Battalion was crossing open grain fields, attracting heavy concentrations of enemy artillery fire.

As we approached the rock quarry, I took cover in some small boulders and brush near the entrance and observed. Corny covered me from twenty or thirty yards behind. An enemy shell came in, and Corny was sure it had fallen right on top of me. Later, he told me that I came to life, shook the dust from my uniform, and told him, "Lets get out of this quarry area!"

We moved to the left, toward the direction where the 3rd Battalion was heavily engaged, searching for a route the company could take around the quarry to get in position for the attack. We found a route that would provide cover and learned that we could follow it to climb to a hilltop just beyond the quarry line. On the hilltop was a short grain field that stretched toward the city of Lanuvio, located high up the hill about a mile away. Corny and I could see the enemy defensive line beyond where the grain field ended and a vineyard began. We would have to assault across 300 to 400 yards of open field in order to seize the first enemy position (see Sketch 11).

Sketch 11

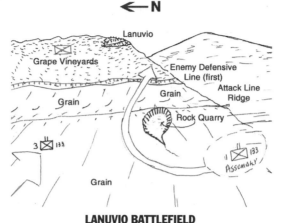

LANUVIO BATTLEFIELD

The next day, I was able to keep Company C out of the quarry for the attack. Instead, I led the company along the general route of my reconnaissance path to get into an attack position.[2]

I moved the company to the attack area under the cover of darkness and deployed two platoons in assault. We were joined in the battle by a platoon of five tank destroyers. Perhaps a sister company was supposed to attack on my right, but in the confusion of battle, I never saw that happen.

Our assault troops began to move forward over the crest of a small ridge, where we came under immediate and intense mortar fire from the Germans.

I had difficulty coordinating the attack with the tank destroyer platoon. I went to each tank, looking, without success, for the platoon leader. At one point, I jumped up on a tank and got it to move to the top of the hill and into a firing position. That action attracted fire from the first defensive line. I never was able to get all five vehicles to fire on my designated target areas. I still think that if the tank platoon had arrived earlier, I could have coordinated the assault with them, and it would have been effective.

[2] *I now assume that most of the remaining battalion used the rock quarry as an attack area, and that is where the heaviest casualties probably occurred.*

The Company C assaulting troops were suffering numerous casualties. I could see one, two, or three men almost continuously leaving the line, a rifle still in their hands; bloodstained arms and shoulders were a common sight. I talked to several of these men and saw their multiple wounds. Fortunately, the wounds were not the deep, penetrating type that could be fatal.

I learned from one of the two lead platoons that Lt. Packard was killed in this action. The New Englander was a top-quality officer who was calm, efficient, and highly admired by his men. His death was a great loss.

The two assault platoons had halted on the slope facing the enemy. Mortar fire was continuous and heavy, and there seemed to be many air bursts, which may have accounted for the type of wounds I was seeing. The mortar fire also hindered the tank destroyers because they had large open turrets that provided no cover for the crew. So our tank-destroyer fire was ineffective. These destroyers were also big targets for the enemy fire observers, meaning that the company took even more enemy fire, which rained down on our soldiers exposed on the ground.

The casualties continued to grow. I had counted about fifteen soldiers who had returned with bloody wounds. They represented about twenty percent of our assaulting force. The attack was stalled; one officer was dead. We had to take action quickly!

I called for Lt. Edwin M. Brown,[3] the weapons platoon leader, to meet me and told him to take charge of the left rifle platoon; I was going to take the right platoon. My plan was for the two of us to rush forward, get the men in the platoons up, race forward while firing our weapons, and seize the enemy position, which lay about 200 yards away. I got a single tank destroyer to fire, which assisted us in carrying out my plan.

[3] *Lt. Brown was a West Virginian.*

I rushed to the right and Lt. Brown rushed to the left. As I moved through the dispersed men lying prone on the ground, I yelled, "Get up! Fire your weapons! Lets go!" The men looked up at me in wonder. Somebody was doing something, so up they sprang like rockets, and we all raced forward. I looked to my left and saw that Lt. Brown was having the same good results. As I looked again at Brown running, I saw his left arm fly off into the air.[4] All of the men swept forward, firing weapons on the run; we seized the enemy line.

Postscript

In 1984, Pvt. Leighton McKeithan told me that I grabbed him when we reached our objective and told him to go up and down the line to count how many men were present. He counted forty or forty-five men, he told me. We had started this battle with about sixty.

Corny recently told me that when I told him, "Let's go!" he raised up quickly on his arms and legs and at that instant an enemy bullet struck the ground under his just-raised body.

---

[4] *Lt. Brown survived the war. Later, when I visited him in the hospital, he said he was happy the Germans didn't take his drinking arm!*

11

Around Rome and the Pursuit to the North
Italy, 1944

Rome falling and the D-Day invasion of Normandy, France, were joyous events to the men of Company C. But while U. S. troops celebrated on the fringes of Rome, we crossed the River Tiber in the southwest corner of the ancient city. Our men waded perhaps 200 yards across a stretch of water during the night of 4-5 June 1944.

Once across the Tiber, we walked all night to the northwest, towards the port city of Civitavecchia, which is on the coastal highway. At midmorning, we hailed a column of advancing light reconnaissance tanks and all climbed aboard for better transportation than our feet and legs could give us.

We passed through Civitavecchia early that afternoon and saw the German "Anzio Express" railway guns—280-mm— that the retreating Germans had abandoned in this port area. By nightfall, we had advanced about twenty miles further north to a river where a blown bridge stopped our tanks. We parted from the tanks, which needed to search for crossing sites upstream to our right. At dawn the next morning, we stood at the blown bridge and looked north on Highway 1. What we saw is depicted in Sketch 12.

Sketch 12

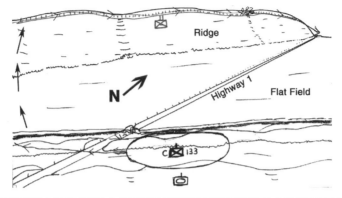

COMPANY C DESTROYS A GERMAN INFANTRY BATTALION, 6-7 JUNE 1944

The view was amazing, and what made it so was that the Germans had built a defensive line on top of the ridge, along its entire length, the first hastily built defensive line we had seen in the war. One could easily see the fighting positions on the top of the ridge since the fresh dirt had not been camouflaged or removed. I was able to count the enemy positions and easily concluded that we were looking at an enemy of battalion strength, perhaps 400 to 500 men. They outnumbered us by at least three to one.

The sight made my blood run hot! Company C was looking at its easiest enemy target ever, and I quickly issued orders. The company was to move downstream and attack the ridge from the German right flank and then sweep down the ridge, destroying the entire German force in one blow.

I wanted some artillery to cover the flanking movement, but none was available since we were too far in front of the entire 5th Army to have any artillery support. I figured that most army troops were probably still in Rome celebrating the fall of the city.

Walking back a bit and looking for some of the light tanks that had brought us to this position, I spotted not the light tanks, but heavy Sherman tanks. I ran to the tanks and located the tank of the company commander, an army captain. I had to jump up on his tank since he wanted to stay completely inside the turret. I told him to move his tanks forward a bit since they were hidden behind hills and said that I wanted his tanks to fire in support of my infantry attack.

My very simple request turned into a duel of wills. The tank captain said that he had to take his force back to the rear. When I asked the reason he was going to the rear, he answered that they needed gasoline. I told him that if he had enough gas to travel twenty miles to the rear, he had sufficient gas to go just 200 yards up to the river and fire in support. He then said that he had to go the rear to get tank ammunition!

Since I was on top of the tank looking down into the turret at the captain, I could see that he was surrounded with rounds of ammunition. I was sure that his force had not had any occasion to fire on the enemy for the past few days and challenged him on the ammunition. This time, he said he had to go back to get high explosive ammunition because all he had was armor piercing ammunition! In my opinion, I had one course of action left. I pulled out my 45 pistol and cocked it, which got his total attention. After that, everything began to work out very well for Company C.

The reluctant captain moved his tanks forward, and I gave him my fire plan and targets. The entire enemy position along the ridge was to be directly fired upon, distracting the Germans so our troops could move down the river and attack the enemy flank. When our infantry reached the ridge and was attacking the enemy positions, the tank fire was shifted to concentrate on supporting our assault, firing at a right angle to the direction of our infantry attack, which swept down the top of the ridge.

It was a beautiful assault. The tank fire was devastating. At times, it lifted the enemy soldiers right out of their fighting holes. Company C infantry bolted along the ridge top at full speed and took the entire ridge by advancing to where the highway crossed the ridge about a mile from the river.

We completely destroyed nearly an entire battalion of German infantry with no losses to ourselves. The enemy was a bicycle infantry battalion that had left Denmark a couple of weeks before. They were completely annihilated. Gone! Now we had the bicycles!

I stayed with the tanks the entire time and thanked the tank company commander for his vital and very effective fire support. Company C and the tank company had been magnificent. After the battle, we rode the German bicycles further along the highway to the north. That night, the 91st Infantry Division relieved us.

Postscript

In 1984, I visited this 1st Battalion battle spot with some of the men in my company. The sketch in this chapter is based on a photo taken at the scene on that trip. I know firsthand what happened in the Company C battle area on the left of the highway, but I think that the battalion also attacked to the right of the highway. I have no recollection of that part of the battle or how it was coordinated with our attack.

12

Company C Battles for Cecina
Italy, 1944

We moved north on the west coast of Italy toward Berlin and approached the coastal city of Cecina, Italy. The coastal highway ran through the city, and the Cecina River flowed westerly through the town and entered into the Mediterranean Sea, about two miles from the city.[1]

The Germans made a determined defense along the Cecina River against our forces.

The capture of Cecina was the objective of the 1st Battalion, and a direct frontal attack was ordered. Coastal Highway 1 would be the left boundary, with Company A on the left and Company C on the right.

The attack took place on 30 June or 1 July 1944. By late afternoon on the day before the battle, Company C had advanced in a column of three rifle platoons (see Sketch 13) between points 1 and 2. The weapons platoon and company headquarters were located at point 3.

I was not satisfied with the deployment. I wanted the rifle

---

[1] *We also visited and photographed this battlefield in 1984. Cecina, which is not a big city, is nestled in slightly rolling hills. It has numerous draws, all covered with lush trees and vegetation. Small streams flow through the draws and pour into the Cecina River.*

platoons heading toward Cecina, but they were heading north rather than northwest. The draw to their left was wide, deep, and covered with trees. It looked menacing, and I feaared it could serve as an avenue for the Germans to attack us. I especially didn't want to enter into it with just a few hours of daylight left. Therefore, I halted the platoons and told them to "hunker down" for the night.

Sketch 13

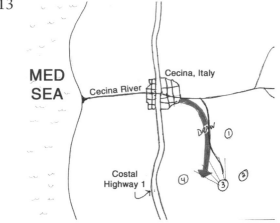

COMPANY C, 133RD INFANTRY, DESTROYS ENEMY ATTACK, CECINA, 1 JULY 1944

I knew that Company A on the other side of the draw from us had been hit rather hard, so I knew we would face a determined enemy. I was concerned about the large draw in my zone because I knew it presented an ideal approach route for a major enemy counterattack that could split the battalion. The draw was a low area that drained the land beside the higher slopes on each side of it.

As night approached, Corny and I entered the draw to see what the enemy was up to. We soon found out! As we moved into the draw several hundred yards, we heard Germans a short distance away, talking quietly and moving around, making the sounds we made ourselves when we were preparing to make an attack. A file of enemy soldiers, moving south probably to attack our troops, walked by us as we lay in a ditch. They were so close to us that we could have tripped them with our hands! At a pause in the noise and enemy movements, we silently withdrew from the draw, returning to its head (point 3).

Corny and I alerted all of the command to the probable enemy counterattack, which I guessed would come at dawn. We told the company headquarters people and the weapons platoon people to expect the attack to come right at them. To our front, the land was rolling and clear, except for small haystacks scattered about a small field.[2] I had the machine guns cover the field and company headquarters cover the draw approach that was in front of us.

We waited all night. At early dawn, I detected movement from the woods into the open field. I alerted the two machine guns, which were positioned side-by-side about twenty yards apart, to be ready. As I watched, I saw soldiers moving from one haystack to another, always stopping behind them[3] for concealment. I had kept the machine-gun-section sergeant by my side and told him to prepare to fire on my orders. My plan was to let the Germans get real close to us so I could have a killing zone all over that small field.

The sergeant whispered to me, "Sir, they are friendly troops."

"No, sergeant," I answered. "American troops would never stop on the north side of each haystack. Be ready to fire!"

We let the first line of enemy troops advance to less than fifty yards from us. In the dim light, the enemy did not know we were ready for them.

"Fire!" I ordered! All weapons cut loose. Even members of company headquarters, who seldom had chances to fire their weapons in battle, cut loose in a deadly barrage of carbine fire.

The enemy never had a chance to recover. They could not mount an advance further into our position and fell back

---

[2] *In 1984, this area was a vineyard.*

[3] *The north side.*

toward Cecina.[4] We had been completely prepared for this enemy counterattack. After the Germans retreated, I moved all of the company diagonally to the left to cut the coastal highway, and we moved forward.

In the early afternoon, the troops rested on the high roadway banks. While we were resting, a comical event occurred. Up the road from the south came an empty 6 x 6 supply truck with two soldiers in the front seat. These soldiers wove their truck between many shell-blown tree branches and stopped to talk to some of our men. "Have you boys seen the front lines?" they asked. Now, asking a soldier if he has seen the front line when he *is* the front line is asking for trouble!

The raw answer came out, "Naw, we haven't seen it."

The truck moved forward, and immediately a burst of enemy machine-gun fire came from the north. The truck almost seemed to rear up on its back wheels; then it turned around and headed south at a rapid speed, crashing through the large branches scattered in the road.

The truck's occupants must have ducked for cover because all we could see was a pair of hands on the steering wheel! Fortunately, they made it safely out of there. Surely they had seen the front lines!

Scene of the battle.

---

[4] *In recent years, Capt. Gordon of Company A told me that we saved his company with that fire since the enemy would have hit his flank. Perhaps that was what the Germans had in mind.*

13

Battles of Late June and July
Italy, 1944

I can't remember all of the events of late June and July 1944, so I will cover only those highlights that I can recall.

Company C experienced more successes offensively than ever before. The German opposition helped because their delaying tactics, even if they pressed upon our force every day and not from any defined defensive line, allowed us to maneuver and move rapidly to their flanks and rear.

The company had just about the right number of men to be efficient. The strength of our force was about 125 to 140 men, not the 176 we were allowed. In mountain warfare, 125 men can move quicker than 170 men. One has sufficient firepower with 125 men when they are as seasoned as these veterans were. The men were superb. The officers and non-commissioned officers were aggressive, and all functioned professionally as a unit. We had a good cadre of platoon leaders.

The hasty defenses the Germans put up played into our hands. Prior to an attack, my reconnaissance effectively learned the location of the enemy—and its strength. I could find the enemy machine guns in no time because the Germans repeated their methods over and over again: they placed their main guns high on small mountains so they could re-supply or pull them out as necessary. I could guess the enemy's strength on a mountain to within ten to fifteen percent of his force. We could maneuver the company to flanks and to the rear of the enemy with ease. So many attacks were made that now my memory just cannot pick them up.

I issued attack orders, at times, to the platoon leaders based on my estimate of enemy strength; multiply that strength by the number of Italian lira each German would normally carry and call it a certain amount of lira or a certain amount of dollars objective. The Italian money could be spent by our troops, too. This was a "fun" incentive. My directive to the officers was to divide the lira among our troops. The officers were not to share in any of the proceeds. At times we took $400 mountains![1]

We had good officers, but it is difficult for me to remember their names; I wish I could. I hope that they will forgive me. However, I do remember one lieutenant in particular: "Buck" Taylor from Empire Mine Valley in California. He was a tall, lanky Westerner who resembled Gary Cooper. He was slightly older than most of us, knew how to fight, and handled a platoon with expertise. The fighting power of his platoon was twice that of other platoons. He could be seen on the battlefield, moving around like a Stonewall Jackson on foot. Buck ordered sergeants to move squads precisely where he wanted them to go, always in a way that allowed them to deliver support fire for each other. During an assault, he was in the midst of his men as they charged the enemy at close quarters.

I also remember the "battalion problem" I had each day. I received an order in overlay form[2] giving me the job of taking the next day's assigned battalion objectives. I had no staff, as the battalion had, so it was a real burden to reconnoiter the entire battalion front, direct three rifle companies to attack, coordinate fires and support, and take care of all the details necessary for success. Handling these jobs became a habit and,

---

[1] *Our soldiers got one or two dollars a day, as pay, so this was big money then.*

[2] *An overlay is placed over a contour map and shows the battle lines of units, the directions of attack, and similar information.*

fortunately, I got results. I could carry out my orders, but it took a lot of time and effort to bear that extra responsibility. I'm sure that this extra load helped blur my memory of events during this period.

However, four events do stand out in my memory. For one attack, I ordered a double envelopment of a mountain objective. I got Corny, who was a very brave soldier, to go with me up the middle of the mountain so I could coordinate the final attack. The two of us moved all the time as a team; I would cover him as he moved, and, likewise, he would cover me as I moved. But I had a problem here with Corny. He wanted to go first all of the time, and I insisted that we share it on a fifty/fifty basis. Sometimes he would fake me out by saying he had found a new and better route and would shove off in front again. To pay him back, I would sometimes pull the same thing on him, which I did as we climbed almost straight up, grabbing branches of bushes to help get up the steep slopes. I spotted a small clearing to the right of our course and shoved off in front. I had my carbine strapped over my shoulder since I had used both hands to help me climb. Suddenly, I walked into a hidden German machine-gun position. Fortunately for me, the Germans were not in a firing position, but they were scrambling to get to their weapon. I hit the ground and yelled at Corny to pull his pistol and fire over me, which he did in fast Texas fashion. He accomplished the deed, saving me.

My memory also clicks when recalling the day of 11 July 1944. 1 had had a nightmare while we were in North Africa a year or so before that date. I had dreamed that I was in a large hole in the ground and was killed by an enemy shell on 11 July 1944. When that day actually arrived, that nightmare was on my mind, believe me, throughout the day!

As the day progressed, we attacked the saddle of a hill, which was located between two mountains, that had a ruined ancient castle perched on it. My reconnaissance showed no enemy positions, so I attacked with a column of platoons. The lead platoon swept over the ridge saddle and continued to the far north side, where the enemy hit them in a rear slope defense, which we could not see before we made the attack.

We suffered casualties. I called for the Germans to allow both sides to hold a cease-fire in order to get our wounded men off the battlefield. The Germans agreed to the cease-fire but stipulated that they, themselves, would administer first-aid. In horror, we watched as two Germans came forward and knelt down by a wounded American soldier and then shot him. Immediately, I ordered fire to destroy the two Germans. The enemy troops were SS, or storm troopers, and their vile act illustrated the lack of ethics and humanity of at least some SS troops.

We pulled back to the basement of the castle ruins to reorganize the platoon, and I realized that the basement was the hole in the ground of my dream! The Germans continually dropped artillery rounds all around us but kept missing our "hole." Even one shell would have been fatal to many of us.

A few days later, we were involved in another attack at a town whose name I can no longer recall. The battalion plan was that B and C Companies would attack at 4:00 a.m. from the town. Both companies were to meet at a street corner, right by battalion headquarters. We awakened at 2:00 a.m., ate breakfast, and prepared for the attack. At 4:00 a.m., I led the company in column formation to the meeting point. We were on time, but Company B was nowhere in sight.

I went into the nearby battalion headquarters to get instructions and found a very bad situation. Both the battalion and B Company commanders were dead drunk and passed out on the floor side-by-side. I conferred with the duty officer, and we both felt it was important to keep pressure on the Germans, not giving them time to improve their defenses. I decided to attack and obtained approval from the operations officer.

C Company set out under cover of darkness in a single file to the top of a ridge, which was north of the village. We moved silently through a probable outpost line and continued to move swiftly forward for nearly one and a half hours, riding the crest of a north-south running ridge that was about a quarter of a mile wide. A similar ridge lay to our east. At first light, I was able to see large, square farmhouses on the east ridge, about half a mile apart. As the light increased, I spotted large wooden shutters on the huge second-story windows that were slowly being opened in the now visible farmhouses.

Sketch 14

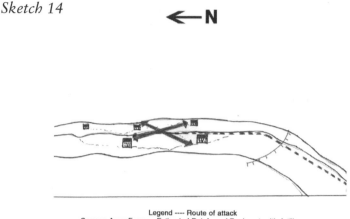

Legend ---- Route of attack
German Army Forces - Estimated Reinforced Regiment, with Artillery

COMPANY C ROUTS A LARGE ENEMY FORCE LATE JULY 1944

I knew that the Germans surrounded us. We were certainly out-numbered and could be destroyed, so we had to fight our way out of this situation. I called the platoon leaders forward and issued quick attack orders: "Company C is surrounded by a regiment of Germans.[3] Company C will attack and act like an American regiment. We will attack from the center spot where I stand and attack in a 360-degree direction."[4] I divided the terrain visually into three pie slices of 120 degrees each and put our weapons—machine guns and mortars—in the center of the pie. When all of the troops had moved into the attack positions I had designated, I would then order fire, and all weapons of all of the men in the company would begin firing. The platoons would fire and move forward; then they would halt on my order. My ruse for attacking the Germans had to work quickly

---

[3] *That was only my guess, but it turned out to be true.*

[4] *In other words, I ordered the company to attack in all directions.*

since it was getting somewhat lighter but still not light enough for the enemy to see us moving to our attack positions.

On my command, we opened fire simultaneously, and the riflemen moved forward, firing as fast as they could. We did sound like a regiment! The ruse worked like magic. The Germans on all sides of us were completely surprised. They left in droves—artillery units pulled out; trucks with infantry soldiers pulled out; they retreated in haste.

I stopped the troops' movement after about a 150-yard advance but kept up the firing. The battle was over in a short ten minutes. We didn't damage the enemy, but we surely put fear into them. In the process, we saved ourselves because in another few minutes we would have been discovered and probably attacked by a much superior force. All-in-all, I got us into that situation—and I believe I got us out of it!

By then, we had penetrated deep within enemy lines—perhaps a two-mile thrust. That in itself must have concerned the Germans because they pulled out in such haste. Again, we were way out in front of all of the 5th Army troops. As had happened before, my battalion commander seems to have had a problem in reporting our successful attack. To my knowledge, it was never reported to the regiment.

Another event during this period was an attack by C Company on a castle complete with surrounding wall and moat. We had forged across the moat and up to the wall. Our problem then was to get through the entrance gate and storm the castle itself, just fifty yards from the entrance in the wall. Surely, I thought, the defending Germans would concentrate their firing on this entrance.

Help came to us from an unexpected source—from the heavens in the form of a flight of P-51 Mustangs, twelve planes in all.[5] Another regimental unit, which was attacking another

---

[5] *At a July 1991 reunion in Richmond, Virginia, Pvt. 1st Class Harry Davidson shared his recollections with me. He said that he was also up against the castle wall when he looked up at the afternoon summer sky and saw a plane diving at us with bombs hung on the wings. He did not know if the plane was enemy or friendly until the bombs fell on the castle fifty yards from him.*

castle nearby, had called for air support and had arranged to use smoke to mark their castle. We had, as usual, fought hard, thrown smoke grenades, and used our mortar fire to help us get to the gate. Our own battle and the ensuing smoke had been seen by our new-found friends as a target for them. I would like to think we made more smoke than had the other unit.

Nonetheless, we really benefited. We probably had the closest air support of any rifle company in World War II. All twelve planes hit the castle. When we moved in, we found some live, but dazed, Germans deep in the basement. Pvt. 1st Class Harry Davidson later told me that a captured German officer described the Americans as crazy for calling for such close air support. Maybe so, but that "craziness," misdirected though it was, saved American lives.

14

"Magnificent Troops"
Italy, 1944

Along with the entire 34th Division, Company C spent a peaceful period at Rosignano, by the sea, as the 5th Army reserve division. It was a well-deserved rest for this veteran group of warriors.

A most memorable event took place on 11 August 1944.[1] We learned that the company would be visited by a "very prominent person"—and it turned out to be an historic moment for all of us. We assembled by a dirt road; I had the men go to a rushing mountain stream we had passed to wash the mud from their boots and helmets. When they returned to the road, I had them to stand tall in company-front formation, with the tallest men in the front ranks.

A jeep dashed toward us with Gen. Clark, commanding general of the 5th Army, in the back seat and the very prominent person to the right of the driver. Gen. Clark leaped from the vehicle before the jeep stopped. I had ordered Company C to present arms and then saluted the general, reporting, "Capt. Wilkinson, commander of Company C, 133rd Infantry Regiment, reports to the commanding general, 5th Army."

Gen. Clark returned my salute, and the VIP moved in front of me as the general said, "Cap. Wilkinson, I present the Prime Minister of Great Britain."

I saluted Sir Winston Churchill, and he extended his hand to shake mine. After we shook hands, Sir Winston spoke, " Captain, I

[1] *My memory tells me that Company C still had not been relieved from our front-line duty. Harry Davidson recalled the same thing, even before I told him what my memory led me to believe.*

would like to inspect your troops,"

" Sir, the honor is ours," I replied.

I ordered the men to "prepare for inspection," then to "order arms," and finally to "open ranks, march." I had not issued these latter orders in our year and a half of combat. But the troops smartly executed my orders, and Sir Winston, General Clark, and I began to move down each line of troops—three of them. Sir Winston spoke individually to each man in the company. After speaking to the last man and prior to his departure, the Prime Minister told me that I commanded "magnificent troops!"[2] My heart and mind told me Sir Winston had said the right thing. Truly these were magnificent troops.

Churchill drove by to review other 34th Division troops, but Company C was the only unit that he inspected.[3]

After this experience, it came my time to leave the troops. I had promised the original group that I would stay with them until the last original member of the group had left, either to go home on leave status or to be permanently transferred. The last man to leave was the division-rear clerk, who faithfully fulfilled the necessary administration duties, many miles to the rear, in real comfort compared to these front-line veterans. When he left, I decided to leave also.

I assembled the troops to tell them that I was moving from the company to the battalion, where I would be the battalion executive officer. I would not be far away from them. I wished them the best and told them that based on a recent assassination attempt on the life of dictator Adolph Hitler, I hoped the war would not last much longer and that their own self-applied goals to soon go home would be fulfilled.[4]

---

[2] *Again, my memory was verified by Harry Davidson, who had been standing nearby and said he heard Sir Winston Churchill make a rewarding statement about the men of this company.*

[3] *Churchill's visit to the 34th Division, the only U. S. division he visited, was to show his respect for the sole U. S. Infantry Division that had fought with the British Army in Tunisia and Italy.*

[4] *In retrospect, I was too optimistic and too hopeful for all of them. It would take another eight months of combat before the war ended for these brave men.*

Company C in the Gothic Line
North of Florence, Italy, 1944

The 5th Army had its sights on the city of Bologna across the Apennine mountain mass from Florence, Italy. Bologna was sitiuated in the Po Valley, and the Germans and the Apennines blocked our way.

The 133rd Infantry Regiment was on the left of the division's attack. The V Battalion took Legri, located about twenty miles north of Florence. Riding in a jeep, Maj. Dumont and I swept into a town near the base of the Apennines, and from a house on the southern side of the town, we directed the artillery and infantry that attacked the enemy, who held houses to the north of the town. We took the town.

As the 1st Battalion entered the German Gothic Line, fierce fighting took place. I was overseeing the troops and perceived that Company C was having some difficulty in the battalion attack on Mount Meggiore.

I took Corny with me to see what assistance we could provide and spotted an enemy machine-gun nest on the hill mass to the right and on the flank of the company. That weapon inhibited our soldiers from advancing since it was firing into the company's flank.

Corny and I carefully approached an empty stone farm building on the flank that could offer us a bit of protection and could provide us with a site for firing on the enemy gun.

When we reached the farmhouse wall, we saw a dead G1, his rifle by his side. I grabbed his M-1 rifle and went into the building. Corny and I both entered a room on the second floor that had a window facing the enemy gun. I knelt in the middle of the room, gave Corny my field glasses, and told him to get behind me so he could correct my firing of the M-1 rifle at the target, which was some 200 to 300 yards away.

When I aimed at the machine gun and fired, we both were dismayed to see the rifle shoot a tracer shell rather than regular ball ammunition. We were extremely surprised when, just as I had finished shooting at the enemy, a burst of machine-gun fire came through the window, missing me by an inch or so but hitting Corny! Obviously, the enemy gunner had seen our tracer shot.

Corny caught a bullet across the right side of his chest. I patched him up and got him out of there as quickly as possible. He was tough, and even as a patient, he was a good walker—and even runner—as we left to find aid for him.[1]

Corny was the bravest of the brave. We got each other through the war!

I returned to Company C that night to see what help I could provide. I found the company quite disorganized, and the men, who were spread out, didn't know where their leaders were. I finally found a man who knew the location of the officers, and he took me to to them in a bunker just inside enemy lines. As I walked into this dank bunker, someone recognized my voice, and the group of three or four officers stood up and came to attention.

In the dim interior light, I could see most of the company officers. I addressed them very carefully with these points: "The

---

[1] *In post-war life, Corny has been successful in a nursery business in Houston, Texas. He recalls that I asked soldiers to make a stretcher for him, and he was carried to the rear under heavy mortar fire. He was carried to a rocky field with many other wounded soldiers, and he was the first of the wounded men to be loaded onto an evacuation plane. In Rome, maybe 500 miles away, surgeons operated on his bloody wound that afternoon. In eleven days he was well enough to return to his work.*

men are scattered; the sergeants must find their men; the officers must get reports from their sergeants. We will attack tonight."

I called battalion headquarters to request that I be transferred from battalion executive officer to commander of Company C. My request was approved as was my proposal to attack.

In an hour or so, the officers returned to the bunker and reported that the platoons were in attack position and ready to move. I issued the order to attack and emphasized that the attack was not to be stopped even if it took days to plow through the enemy positions. We attacked near midnight with artillery fire in support.

We advanced all night, though the next two days, and into the third day. I ordered a halt as we cut past the high ground of Mount Meggoire and descended the north slopes, slicing into a narrow highway. We were dog-tired. We had taken a three- to four-mile long, south to north mountain ridge. Other troops passed through our ranks that afternoon.

After that, I returned to my position as executive officer of the battalion.

Let me set the scene for the next battle. Ahead of the battalion lay Mount Venere, a formidable mountain that rose like a head above the other "shoulder" mountains.

Sketch 15

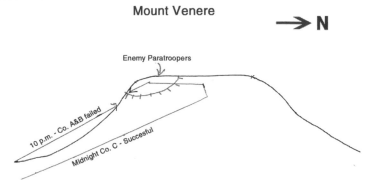

BATTLE FOR MOUNT VENERE, WHERE THE 1ST BATTALION EARNED THE PRESIDENTIAL UNIT CITATION

The 34th Division was under the command of Brig. Gen. Gustaf J. Braun, who had been an active leader. In fact, I saw him on the fighting line, the only time in my fighting career that I had seen a 34th Division general on the fighting line. I was so impressed that I made a point to be with him as we moved forward daily. Gen. Braun was an inspiration to all of us as he calmly walked and talked among the men. He attracted enemy fire because he took no cover, and although the men winced, his presence inspired new confidence in us.

At our battalion post, Gen. Braun took the phone and called Maj. Gen. Bolte, who was at division headquarters, and told the major general that he was putting "Wilkinson in command of the battalion." I was surprised because I had no idea that General Bolte, whom I had never seen, had any idea who I was.

I welcomed the challenge, and Gen. Braun told me to take Mount Venere. I laid plans to advance toward Mount Venere, and we began our approach. The mountainous area made it difficult for the tanks to move, so Gen. Braun verbally pushed them to keep up with the infantry, which aided our advance.

As we approached Mount Venere, I made plans for a night assault in a frontal attack on the mountain, which stood at a height of 3,766 feet. The nearby surrounding mountains reached 2,000 feet in elevation. We had no roads to follow as we headed north, only a single trail that headed to the right of the mountain.

My plan was to have A and B Companies attack side-by-side at night and to seize the heights. I kept Company C in reserve, placing them to the right of the battalion on the east side of the mountain and near the attack area. If I needed their help, I wanted them to have the shortest distance possible to begin an attack.

The commanders of Companies A and B were new replacement officers. Both were captains with no prior combat experience, which was not a helpful situation.

I received the first battle report at about 10:00 p.m. Both companies had been in the assault near the top of Mount Venere. The enemy had countered and had driven both companies back. I immediately ordered Company C to climb the additional 800 feet to reach the top and to envelop the right flank of the enemy. They had to attack the rear of the enemy's position at midnight that night, according to my plan.

I had complete confidence that Company C would seize the top of Mount Venere as I had ordered them to do.

After watching Company C move out and because of my confidence in their ability, I lay on the ground and was able to take a short nap to help prepare myself for what lay ahead. I was awake later to hear Company C's midnight assault.

This was a demanding mission, and I had given it to Lt. Wayne Patrick of Georgia, commander of Company C. It still took skill and determination for the men to move around the enemy without being detected as they climbed the heights. Likewise, most—if not all—of the men moved together and assumed an assault position to finish the vital part of the attack: a violent rush with rifle fire, at midnight, into the enemy's rear. The battle was over in a flash because it was executed so brilliantly.

When I received the report that Company C had seized Mount Venere, it was what I had expected. The company had overpowered an enemy comprised of German 4th Parachute Division soldiers who were veterans of many battles. The men of Company C proudly brought their German prisoners of war to me, and these POWs were as mad as they could be. To be taken by nearly a half-strength rifle company was not what they expected; that must have been one thought in their sullen minds.

Before daybreak, I was on top of Mount Venere with the troops. After dawn broke, we could see the Po Valley and the city of Bologna.

About two miles north of Mount Venere, we could see a ridge with steep slopes to the east and west. The ridge ended in a very steep escarpment on a cliff-like breach about two miles further to the north, which I felt would protect us from a frontal attack. I decided that we should seize the golden opportunity that the escarpment offered.

Thus, I ordered A and B Companies to move north, side-by-side. The day was drizzly and rainy. General Braun joined us on the north slopes of Mount Venere at about 8:00 or 9:00 a.m., and I reported to him on the events of the night and my plans for deep penetration further to the north that morning. He congratulated me in a grand manner for what we had done and told me to advance to the escarpment, which I had shown him on the map.

The War Department later awarded a Presidential Unit Citation to the 1st Battalion of the 133rd Infantry for its capture of Mount Venere. This citation is the equivalent of each man in the battalion receiving the Distinguished Service Cross, the second highest medal for valor next to the Medal of Honor. Company C made it all happen. To my knowledge, this Presidential Unit Citation had been awarded only two or three times to units of the division.

Our move northward for the next two miles drove us deep into the enemy position. In attack, the two companies had strong tendencies to enter buildings to escape the light rain. I ordered both commanders to keep their men out of all buildings and to get moving. I had to tell them a second time before they did it right, but then they followed my orders.

Before noon, we had made the penetration I had desired. It had stopped raining, and we were able to observe more targets for artillery fire than I had ever seen on a battlefield. To our right, across a deep defile and on the next mountain ridge, was our target. We were behind the Germans. We saw artillery batteries, command posts in farm buildings, reserves in movement, ammunition trucks parked up against the back of buildings, and reserves being brought forward.

I had four different artillery forward observers who stood in line for their orders to attack these prime targets. The fourth in line was a British major. "Sir, what have you got?" I asked.

He said, " Eight-inch U. S. howitzers, but I only have three rounds that I can fire." I had just the target for him—a huge farm building that I surmised was a major command post since it had several command-type vehicles parked against the wall on the north side of the building.

I observed in awe as he executed his orders. The first round was for correction since I had asked for a round of delayed fuse to hit the building. The second round went through the roof and exploded inside the building, and the entire solid-stone building came apart. I told him to give me a third round of surface burst on the vehicles. He moved that third shell about fifty feet further north and it landed right on the vehicles. "Mission accomplished," he said.

I replied, "That was the most accurate artillery firing I have ever seen."

We fired on many enemy targets during that entire afternoon. At the time, we were way out in front of all of the troops of the 5th Army.

This was my last battle of our campaigns in Africa and Europe.

Northwest slope of Mount Venere. Company C attacked the east slope on the opposite side.

Much to my sorrow, Gen. Braun was later killed in action. This news was crushing to me because I had so much respect and admiration for this man. In addition to being a very good soldier, he was my mentor, and I have never forgotten him or what he meant to me.

I elected to go back to the United States since I had sufficient "points" to qualify to return stateside. Just before that, the decision had been made to organize all Allied forces in a winter defense along the Gothic Line. Since defense was not my thing, I departed.

As I was leaving the 34th Division headquarters, an officer in the G-3 (Operations) Office told me of the contribution of the total effort made by Company C. He said that I had commanded a rifle company for more days than any other officer of the division. He also said that at that date, Company C had had 1,970 men and 99 officers to pass through the company and that those men and officers had received 1,440 Purple Heart awards for wounds in action. I hoped that these figures were as low as—or lower than—any other rifle company in the division. Company C had fought very hard for a very long time.

ABOUT THE AUTHOR

Richard Franklin Wilkinson, who is known as "Dick" to his friends and associates, was born in the James City County farming community of Toano, Virginia, in 1921. The Wilkinson family had settled in the county near Jamestown; earliest records show a Wilkinson farm there in 1666. The farm was located at Greensprings, near the site of the first British colonial governor's estate. Richard's grandfather, William M. Wilkinson (1841-1902), was born at Merry Oaks Plantation near Toano. A farmer's son, William Wilkinson served in the 32nd Virginia Infantry and in the 1st Virginia Artillery Regiment from 1861-1865 and fought in numerous Civil War battles.

When Richard was growing up, he led a very active outdoor life, tilling the soil and helping harvest the crops on local farms. He was also a skilled horseman and hunter. In 1938, he enrolled in Virginia Agricultural and Mechanical College and Polytechnic Institute, now Virginia Polytechnic Institute and State University, known popularly as Virginia Tech, where he was a member of the corps of cadets, then comprised of about 2,700 full-time cadets. He volunteered to serve in the infantry battalion at VPI, as the school was popularly known at the time, and became skilled with infantry weapons and tactics. He graduated in 1942 with a bachelor's degree in forestry.

Richard Wilkinson entered the U. S. Army in June 1942 and attended the Basic Infantry course at Fort Benning, Georgia, graduating in the summer of 1942. In September 1942, 2nd Lt. Wilkinson joined the 34th Infantry Division, which was stationed in Northern Ireland. He was assigned to Company C, 1st Battalion, 133rd Infantry Regiment.

Wilkinson served as a combat platoon leader and then a company commander in Tunisia and as a company and battalion commander in Italy. All of these duties involved front-line combat during several hundred days of action with the 34th Division.

The book *Dog Faces Who Smiled Through Tears*, written by Homer R. Ankrum, covers in detail the actions of the 34th "Red Bull" Infantry Division in World War II. Homer Ankrum dedicated the book as follows: "For Colonel Richard F. Wilkinson, U. S. A., Retired, one of the most outstanding Company Commanders to serve with the 34th "Red Bull" Infantry Division and one whose brilliant leadership, while commanding the 1st Battalion, 133rd Infantry Regiment, contributed to his battalion's heroic performance that resulted in the award of the Presidential Unit Citation."

Richard F. Wilkinson served in the U. S. Army from 1942 to 1972. During the Cold War (1945-1989), he served in Europe, Japan, Taiwan, Korea, and Vietnam. He was also a paratrooper. He served four years on the faculty of the Command and General Staff College in Fort Leavenworth, Kansas, and nine years in staff positions with major U. S. Navy Seventh Fleet (Vietnam) and joint Army-Navy-Air Force Unified Commands. Additionally, he was a deputy commander of the 6th Infantry troops, who were occupying Berlin along with British and French infantry troops from 1958-1961.

Upon retiring from the Army in 1972 at the age of fifty-one, he became a successful farmer, served in leadership roles in his church, was chairman of the York County Economic Development Authority from 1981-1990, and was active in family business matters.

Col. Wilkinson has always shown a keen interest in the postwar activities of Company C and has written extensively about and has visited all of the battlefields where the company fought during World War II. He has always greatly admired the men with whom he fought.

Col. Wilkinson has been married to Margaret Walton Wilkinson for sixty years. They have four children—Richard Jr., Jane Rice, Thomas Preston, and Nancy Bell—five grandchildren, and two great-grandchildren.

Together Col. And Mrs. Wilkinson have been active in the training and education of retarded citizens. Both have also played active roles in establishing scholarships for cadets at Virginia Tech. Over the years, they have traveled extensively throughout many parts of the globe.

July 1, 2005, Williamsburg, Virginia

Col. Richard F. Wilkinson